STUDIES IN LEGAL TERMINOLOGY

STUDIES IN LEGAL

TERMINOLOGY

By

ERWIN HEXNER, J.D., D.Pol.Sci.

Visiting Professor at the University of North Carolina

CHAPEL HILL
THE UNIVERSITY OF NORTH CAROLINA PRESS
1941

PREFACE

THE FOLLOWING ESSAYS concern a few frequently discussed concepts of the political and legal sciences. To realize that in these politically tempestuous times we are still struggling with old, elementary terminological problems may be bewildering for the first moment. However, often behind what seems to be merely terminological issues there are concealed vital political problems. Different extra-legal views frequently make difficult a common understanding of even very simple legal concepts. In the immediate future these difficulties may increase still more. Thus, political and legal doctrine furnishes a striking analogy to the ziggurat tower of Babel. The confusion of tongues and expressions in this particular field is disconcerting and causes unexpectedly important effects. It was not by accident that Kant, discussing the difficulties in defining terms, referred to jurists who "are still without a definition of their concept of the law."[1] These pages are an attempt to review in a fragmentary and simple manner cer-

[1] *Critique of Pure Reason*, trans. by N. K. Smith (London, 1933). p. 313. Smith translated the term "Recht" as "right."

tain relationships pertaining to those general concepts, comparing some characteristic features of
specific legal orders, but avoiding the attempt to
approach problems pertaining to any particular legal
system.

It is not necessary to emphasize that the literature
quoted represents only a few hints and does not even
include the most authoritative works.

I am greatly indebted to Professor Charles Basker-
ville Robson for many suggestions and for reading
the manuscript and to Mrs. Adelaide Walters for
reading the proofs. My thanks are also due to Miss
Lucile Marshall Elliott, Law Librarian, and to Mrs.
Helen Maltby Lumpkin, Assistant Law Librarian,
of the University of North Carolina for their valuable assistance.

The University of North Carolina,
Chapel Hill, N. C.   E. H.

CONTENTS

STUDIES IN LEGAL TERMINOLOGY

I

RULES CONTROLLING SOCIAL CONDUCT

A MODERN, complex social life requires various heteronomous means of influencing human social conduct.[1] Some of these means are supposed to be arbitrarily created and maintained[2] by human volition;
others are not considered to be subject to arbitrary
creation or change by human will. Even the arbitrarily created means were regarded by Thomas Aquinas
and other authors as proceeding from God. "As to
the design of government, God governs all things
immediately; whereas in its execution, He governs
some things by means of others."[3] He obviously

[1] "It may be the destiny of man that the social instincts shall grow
to control his actions absolutely, even in antisocial situations. But they
have not yet done so. . . . —O. W. Holmes, Jr., *The Common Law*
(Boston, 1881), p. 44.

[2] "For law requires not only law-givers but also law-keepers. . . ."
—Sir Henry Slesser, *The Law* (London, 1936), p. 192.

[3] *Summa Theologica*, Part I, Question 103, Art. 6, trans. by Fa-
thers of the English Dominican Province (London, 1922), V, 14. Cf.
the following opinion of Dr. Roscoe Pound (*A New School of Jurists*,
The University Studies of the University of Nebraska [Lincoln, 1904],
IV, 257): "No conception has been more fruitful in legal history than
this notion that the foundation of law is an ideal or natural justice."
In this connection should be examined the old and renewed doctrine
that a *real* social force is a *legitimate* one, and that, according to
Thomas Aquinas, there is a distinction between "rationis ordinatio"
and mere arbitrariness. "There is no power but from God; and those

viewed *human* legislatures as executive agencies of the government of God in which God vested sub-legislative powers.[4] To be sure, even those means intended to influence human social conduct which are regarded as arbitrarily created by men are subject to many limitations in several dimensions and in various degrees of intensity. Geographical circumstances, physical and psychical properties,[5] and other factors set limits to human will.[6] One of the mightiest among such factors is the belief in a social or individual or combined system of values culminating in the concept of what is called justice.[7] With

that are, are ordained of God (Rom. XIII, 1). . . . All power, therefore, whether of the sovereign or of subordinate authorities, comes from God."—Litt. ency., *Ad Beatissimi Apostolorum Principis* (dated November 1, 1914), *Acta Apostolicae Sedis, 1914*, p. 651. The examination of this doctrine leads necessarily to the question posed by St. Augustine: Non sunt regna nisi magna latrocinia? The famous dialogue between Alexander the Great and the pirate (*De Civitate Dei,* lib. IV, cap. 4) should impress the political scientist now more than ever before.

[4] With reference to the concept of the rulers as the "lieutenants of God," cf. the doctrines of Richelieu, Le Bret, Bossuet, Louis XIV, etc., in Henri Sée, *Les Idées politiques en France au XVIIe siècle* (Paris, 1932), *passim,* and his introduction to *L'Évolution de la pensée politique en France au XVIIIe siècle* (Paris, 1925), pp. 9 ff.

[5] Mr. Justice Holmes (*Collected Legal Papers* [New York, 1921], p. 200) taught: "The law can ask no better justification than the deepest instincts of man."

[6] That is why the appointment of his horse as consul of the Roman Empire by the Emperor Caligula could not become a *legal* rule.

[7] According to N. S. Timasheff (*An Introduction to the Sociology of Law* [Cambridge, 1939], p. 72), "A decision in accordance with law, social ethics, et cetera, can be made without reference to justice. Yet the term designates the element which these decisions have in common, i.e., the property of being based on social ethics (on the social recognition of value systems)." The common belief in justice is strengthened by such expressions as Ministry of Justice, Court of

reference to human regulations, it is misleading but understandable to call these limits "higher laws."[8] Such limits are naturally changed in the process of time. The human will's arbitrary regulation of human social conduct is strongly influenced by several internal and external forces.[9] Modern communication facilities make vain all attempts to establish a mental isolation of and within a nation. The influences of internal and external social forces may be positive or negative; they may put in motion similar or opposing forces.

Facts created and maintained by human volition intended to control human social conduct are either expressed in a specific form of sentences called "rules," or can be transformed by a grammatical operation into rules.[10] Such rules may relate either to

Justice, administration of justice, etc. However, the analysis of what different people regard as just and justice shows why it is necessary "to administer" justice as it happens.

[8] See Duguit, *Traité de droit constitutionnel* (Paris, 1930), III, 709-10. William A. Robson (*Civilisation and the Growth of the Law* [New York, 1935], pp. 329-30) quotes the opinions of Karl Pearson, Charles Singer, and T. W. N. Sullivan, who state that even natural laws are products of the human mind and as such subject to change. W. A. Robson cites Thomas Huxley: "We sought to reconcile juridical law and scientific law by projecting them on to a common plane of function or purpose."—*Ibid.*, p. 335.

[9] "Human life being a perpetual interaction between volition and uncontrollable facts. . . ."—Bertrand Russell, *Power, A New Social Analysis* (London, 1938), p. 265.

[10] Eugen Ehrlich (*Fundamental Principles of the Sociology of Law*, trans. by Walter R. Moll [Cambridge, 1936], p. 40) regarded "Every human relation within the association, whether transient or permanent" as "sustained exclusively by the rules of conduct."

a *particular* person as a social being[11] or group, or
to an *undetermined* person or group. They may relate to a limited or unlimited part of the earth,[12]
and to a limited or unlimited period of time.[13] The
time period to which the rule with reference to the
conduct relates must be a time yet to come, for it
would be meaningless to state that the conduct in
the past should be determined by a rule.

The purport and the interrelation of these social
rules and their enforcement, if any, are generally
adequate for, or at least characteristic of, the social
life in which they are maintained and to which
they relate.[14] Common usage and social science differentiate today among these rules of human social
conduct in accordance with various points of view;
for example, to whom they are attributed,[15] what

[11] See G. Jellinek, *Adam in der Staatslehre* (Neue Heidelberger
Jahrbücher, 1893), I, 135.

[12] Cf. Joseph H. Beale, "The Jurisdiction of a Sovereign State,"
36 *Harv. Law Rev.* 241 ff.; W. W. Cook, "The Logical and Legal
Bases of the Conflict of Laws," 33 *Yale Law Journ.* 457 ff. With reference to the Vatican State, see Cammeo, *Ordinamento giuridico dello
stato della città del Vaticano* (Firenze, 1932), p. 37.

[13] The question of inter-temporal law was discussed in the arbi-
tration between the United States and Holland relating to the Island
of Palmas. See H. Lauterpacht, *Functions of Law in the International
Community* (Oxford, 1933), pp. 283-85. I omit the separate mention
of the problems connected with air navigation, the specific problems
of the maritime law, and the problems pertaining to international
concessions.

[14] Somlo, *Juristische Grundlehre* (Leipzig, 1917), pp. 71-72.

[15] Malinowski (Introduction, p. lxi, to Jan Hogbin, *Law and Order
in Polynesia* [New York, 1934]) expressed a rather skeptical opinion
with reference to the traditional "compendia of comparative ethno-
logical scholarship," writing: "All this material lacks, however, one
thing: that is the fundamental concept of where law or the dynamism
of custom resides in primitive societies."

social relationships and what items of conduct they are concerned with, whether or not they are enforceable by an organized social machine, etc.

Sets of rules essentially dependent upon each other and upon a common center and attributed to the same social force are called "rule systems" or "rule orders." One self-centered set of rules determining social behavior is called a *legal* system or *legal* order. Today there are, besides the legal rule systems, several other rule systems which determine human social behavior: social convention, positive religions, morals, fashion, and so on.[16] In early times there was only one rule system determining human social conduct. The legal rule system has often been considered as segregated from the others.[17] But we have to be aware that even the meaning of a "segregated" legal system presupposes the *coexistence* of other rule systems relating to human social conduct. In other words, there is no *legal* system existing today which is the *only* rule system governing human social conduct. There is a close interconnection and interaction in many dimensions in both a positive and negative sense among the different rule systems which determine human social conduct. Rules recognized as nonlegal rules may cause the creation of

[16] See T. E. Holland, *The Elements of Jurisprudence* (Oxford, 1900), pp. 27 ff.

[17] Roscoe Pound discusses these views in "Fifty Years of Jurisprudence," *Journal of the Society of Public Teachers of Law, 1937*, pp. 29-30.

a new legal rule,[18] or they may cause a new interpretation of an already existing legal rule, and vice versa. We shall discuss the problem of nonlegal rules claiming to be regarded as legal rules later on.[19] We know by experience that there may occur conflicts between certain legal regulations on the one side and human social conventions, fashions, and various other rule systems on the other side. The phrase, "My country—right or wrong!"[20] indicates the possibility of the occurrence of opposing requirements. However, in the majority of cases the different rule systems are, in a positive sense, interactive,[21] in that they support each other.[22] Human conventions may be more strongly supported if expressed through public agencies, for example, the establishing of national specifications as standards

[18] See G. Tarde, *Les Lois de l'imitation* (Paris, Felix Alcan, 1895), pp. 311 ff.

[19] Nonlegal rules may appear in the form of legal rules, and people may comply with them though knowing that they are not *legal*. The reason for such compliance with nonlegal rules may be often found in the lack of *immediate* remedies against such nonlegal acts which appear as legal acts. Besides, people adapt their conduct to certain practices which accompany the legal system but which do not have the character of legal rules.

[20] A phrase not thoroughly analyzed in political doctrine and in ethics.

[21] Cf. Ernst Freund, *Legislative Regulation, A Study of the Ways and Means of Written Law* (New York, 1932), pp. 254 f.; Georg Jellinek, *Allgemeine Staatslehre* (Berlin, 1922), pp. 335-36.

[22] "Let Princes and Rulers of the peoples bear this in mind and bethink themselves whether it be wise and salutary that public authority should divorce itself from the holy religion of Jesus Christ, in which it may find so powerful a support."—Litt. ency., *Ad Beatissimi Apostolorum Principis, Acta Apostolicae Sedis, 1914*, p. 652.

for the measurement, production, or distribution of commodities. Conventions may be supported by setting up a distinction between ordinary unlawful killing of a human being and killing according to human conventions, called the code of dueling. Another example is the fact that the refusal of military service, or at least the service as combatants, by persons who plead conscience has been recognized by the legal orders of the United States and of Great Britain. The interaction may go even further.[23] Several legal orders referring to a moral standard[24] delegate to the moral order sublegislative functions in a figurative sense. The using of other rule systems by the confirmation of statements and the confirmation of allegiance to a legal order by naming God or other sacred things or referring to the conscience, is an old and world-wide instrument employed as an auxiliary in maintenance of a legal system.

The imposition of a "moral embargo" on important commodities or on credit by state authorities is a modern example of this feature. The interrelationship between the legal system and other rule systems may be noticed by observing the effect of

[23] John Stuart Mill in his essay on Liberty (*Utilitarianism, Liberty, and Representative Government* [London, T. N. Dent & Co., 1936], p. 144) did not sympathize with many such interferences by the legal order. See especially his views relating to the prevention of intemperance and the Sabbatarian legislation.

[24] O. W. Holmes, Jr., *The Common Law*, p. 144. See J. L. Kunz, "The 'Vienna School' and International Law," 11 *N. Y. U. Law Quar. Rev.* 390.

mere legal requirements upon the so-called con-
sciences of people. Many people repent even after
successfully evading payment of a custom duty. And
perhaps the most striking example is shown by the
conception of the so-called "conscience money,"
which is sent in Great Britain to the Exchequer by
the repentant evader of the income tax to relieve his
conscience. Positive religions, by expressing as a
commandment, "Thou shalt not steal," refer to the
boundaries of private property as determined by
particular legal orders. That is the reason why this
commandment may have different meanings in
different states. The recognition of an act as
"legal" frequently supplements the internally felt
need of the average man (citizen, public official,
soldier) to investigate whether or not something
that "ought to be done" is "right" or "wrong."

Neither the "body of logically interdependent
rules of law" nor the legal rules as entities exist
as *isolated* units in the social life.[25] But the fact
that the legal system is closely interconnected with
other rule systems does not imply that legal rules
cannot or should not be differentiated from other
rules of conduct. The examination of a legal system as isolated from other rule systems is a very
useful scientific method of study, but its applicability
presupposes that the reader is well informed of the
synoptic presentation of all rule systems influencing

[25] Roscoe Pound, *Fifty Years of Jurisprudence*, p. 18.

social behavior.[26] As a matter of fact, interconnectedness does not exclude the possibility and necessity of distinguishing these things from each other. In states governed according to the totalitarian doctrine, where nearly all human activities are subjected to state regimentation, the differentiation between legal rules and other kinds of rules regulating human conduct is deliberately lessened. Such social systems revert to a much earlier type.[27]

John Dickinson, discussing the different rule systems of human conduct, assumed that one of the systems must be recognized as "ultimate" and that at the present time the "state" is "such a higher source of precepts" from a legal point of view.[28] H. Lauterpacht discussed this "ultimateness" from the point of view of the necessity of protecting "relations which are outside the scope of legal regulations, . . . from interference by, and encroachments of unauthorized force." According to Lauterpacht, "There is in this respect no limitation upon the rule of law in civilized society."[29] Experience shows, on

[26] Professor Roscoe Pound writes that "the political and juristic preaching of today leads logically to absolutism."—*Contemporary Juristic Theory* (Claremont College, 1940), p. 9. I suppose that the non-recognition of the essential interrelationship of the rule systems determining human social behavior is one of the reasons why some political and legal doctrines consciously and unconsciously furnish arguments for absolutism.

[27] See N. S. Timasheff, *op. cit.*, pp. 199, 351.

[28] "A Working Theory of Sovereignty," 42 *Pol. Sc. Quar.* 535. Cf. H. J. Laski, *A Grammar of Politics* (New Haven, 1925), pp. 69-70, quoted by Dickinson.

[29] *Op. cit.*, pp. 390-91.

the one hand, that the modern concept of the state
and the legal order connects the conception of such
a potential "ultimateness" with the ability of the
state to determine its own jurisdiction (compétence
de compétence); and on the other hand, that the
practical exercising of that "ultimate" power over
all areas of human activities (as in a totalitarian system) destroys characteristics which have been traditionally inherent in the concept, "legal" system.

Legal and social sciences have devoted much
energy to the examination of the difference between
legal and moral rules.[30] However, there is no satisfactory and systematic treatment of the interrelationship and interaction among the various social rule
systems.

It is not always determinable whether an item of
human behavior is the direct or indirect consequence
of heteronomous rules of conduct, and if it is,
whether of a legal rule, or another rule belonging to
a nonlegal rule system, or whether of both.

The word "rule" is used in this paper to designate
a hypothetical state of things in the future[31] (reckon-
ing from the time of the creation of the rule) which
ought to be attained.[32] However, the concept of the

[30] Cf. Roscoe Pound, *Contemporary Juristic Theory*, pp. 51-52, and
his *Law and Morals* (Chapel Hill, 1926), *passim*.

[31] "For the laws that concern subjects one amongst another, being
to direct their actions, may well enough precede them."—John Locke,
Of Civil Government, Book II, Chap. XII.

[32] Charles H. Wilson (50 *Law Quar. Rev.* 476) does not use the
expressions "rule" and "norm" as synonyms in the legal sense. "The

term "legal rule" contains some additional elements. The word "rule" applies to the required conduct of men as members of human society and to the desired uniform or corresponding social conduct of several people. Such an "ought-to-be" conduct may be determined by the rule directly or indirectly, and it may be done in general terms or in detail.[33]

In this determination the entrance of other factors may be provided for, as, for example, the volition of certain people in the sense of a directed choice. "Here the law simply authorizes," according to A. Kocourek.[34] Also, "rule" does not designate in this

norm is the expression of a will; it is not the manifestation of knowledge."—H. Kelsen, *Legal Technique in International Law* (Geneva, 1939), p. 20. However, Kelsen did not mean "will" in a psychological sense.

[33] Dean Roscoe Pound is right in opposing the conception of a legal rule as essentially "attaching *definite, detailed* consequences to *definite, detailed* states or situations of fact" and the concept of a "*rigidly constrained* process of adjustment and regulation governed in every detail."—Quoted from Roscoe Pound, *Contemporary Juristic Theory*, p. 11, my italics. General legal rules, especially rules determining the jurisdiction of agencies, do not contain such definite and detailed regulations. However, I suppose that the statement of E. Bodenheimer (*Jurisprudence* [New York, 1940], p. 280) that "The analytical jurist is usually convinced that the legislator has provided a general rule of law for every situation which can possibly arise within a given legal order and that there are no gaps which must be filled in by free judicial discretion" requires some elucidation. I do not want to discuss here the question (it has been discussed many times) whether or not the category "analytical jurists" is very fortunate, but I assume that the concept of "judicial" discretion implies the *legal* limits of this discretion. Within those limits judicial discretion may be called "free." However, none of the analytical jurists mentioned by Bodenheimer would deny that. Dr. Roscoe Pound referred in his statement just cited to the analytical jurists of the last century.

[34] *An Introduction to the Science of Law* (Boston, 1930), p. 248.

paper dominant customs in the past or present, unless they are specifically significant from the point of view here discussed. Nor does the expression "rule" here apply to facts which we expect to happen in nature on a basis of former experience.

Human conduct is determined by legal rules as they are, not by legal rules as somebody would like them to be, i.e., as they ought to be.[35] The form and content of legal rules as they should be belong to the realm of what is called "legal policy." It is a rather involved psychological question whether and how far wishful thinking may be deliberately eliminated from mental operations. Probably in what is called the processes of "understanding," "interpretation," and "verification," there is often a portion of wishful thinking. Even this assumed property of human reasoning does not imply that we should not differentiate clearly between what a legal rule is and what should be the content of it. The correction of legal rules as they are in consideration of what they ought to be is not a proper function of the judicial officer, nor of the administrative officer, nor of the law-abiding citizen in any of these several capacities, except in so far as discretion is legally conferred upon them for this purpose. Even the fact that legal rules are, according to their very nature, more or less flex-

[35] Lon L. Fuller discussed this problem in "Williston on Contracts," 18 *N. C. Law Rev.* 8 ff. Professor Fuller represents an opinion different from that expressed here. Dean Wigmore distinguished clearly "Nomostatics" from other branches of legal sciences.

ible does not imply a transition between "are" and "ought-to-be" rules.

The equivocality of the terms "rule," "law," "standard," etc., has been the reason for many misunderstandings.[36] Natural and social scientists are compelled to explain at the beginning of each paper what they mean when they use these terms.[37] Karl Pearson, discussing in his *Grammar of Science* the meaning of the word "law," emphasized that, because "two quite distinct ideas unfortunately bear the same name, we ought, in order to avoid confusion, to rename one of them or, failing this, we ought, on all occasions, to be quite sure in which of the two senses we are using the name." Pearson was perhaps too pessimistic when he stated "that it would be hard to replace it [the term "law"] now." And he asked, in a manner which is significant for such scholarly disputes, "why is it the scientist rather than the jurist who is to surrender his right to the word?"[38]

[36] N. S. Timasheff (*op. cit.,* pp. 79 f.) distinguished between ethical rules and technical rules.

[37] The sentences designating the meaning of these terms have not "the same intentional significance" required for a common understanding. "A proposition," wrote W. M. Urban, treating the problem of linguistic validity, "is a class of sentences which have the same intentional significance for everyone who understands them. It is this common understanding which makes the proposition."—*Language and Reality* (London, 1939), p. 170.

[38] (London, J. M. Dent & Sons, 1937), pp. 72-73. The British philosopher, F. C. S. Schiller (*How is "Exactness" Possible?* [paper presented to the International Congress of Philosophy in Prague, 1935], p. 1), wrote: "Experience shows that it is quite impossible to pin any philosophic term down to any single meaning, even for a little while, or even to keep its meaning stable enough to avoid gross mis-

I agree with Pearson that "We sadly need separate terms for the routine of sense-impressions, for the brief descriptions or formula of science, and for the canon of social conduct, or, in other words, for the perceptive order, and prescriptive order."[39]   John Austin[40] called attention to the specific difficulties which arise in this connection in examining the conception of the so-called "unwritten law."

The term "law" is also often used in the same sense as I use the expression "legal rule" here. But sometimes the word "law" is used to designate one or several legal rules comprising the same written document. "Law" is used also as a term for such groups of legal rules as common law and criminal law, and the word "law" often denotes all legal systems as an abstraction: the Law.[41] The expression

understanding." I suppose that such problems can be solved only by a co-operative effort of scholars, as recommended by John Dewey ("Unity of Science as a Social Problem," *International Encyclopedia of Unified Science*, I, No. 1, 29 ff.). See also Charles H. Titus, "A Nomenclature in Political Science," 25 *Amer. Pol. Sc. Rev.* 45 ff., 615 ff.

[39] *Op. cit.*, p. 83. Cf. L. Le Fur's report ("Le but du droit," *Yearbook of the Institute Internationale for Legal Philosophy and Juridical Sociology, 1937-1938* [Paris, 1938], p. 4, in further footnotes cited as *Report*) which contains the following proposition: ". . . the law speaks in the imperative mood and not in the indicative mood as the sciences of physical nature do." See Karl L. Llewellyn, "A Realistic Jurisprudence—The Next Step," 30 *Col. Law Rev.* 439.

[40] *Lectures on Jurisprudence* (London, 1879), I, 172. Cf. Pearson, *op. cit.*, p. 73.

[41] With reference to the conception of the law as unchangeable in the process of time and with reference to the modern doctrines which attach "absolute" epithets to the concept of the law, see Arnold Brecht, "The Search for Absolutes in Political and Legal Philosophy," 7 *Social Research* 201-8.

"law" corresponds to the Latin expression "lex," whereas there is no proper English word for the Latin expression "jus."[42] The word "right" expresses only one particular meaning of the Latin term "jus."[43] A further difficulty arises when one seeks a corresponding word in German, Hungarian, and some other languages for the English word "statute." This word is translated into German by the word "Gesetz,"[44] whereas the word "Statut" in German means mainly rules and groups of rules created by public and private "self-governing" corporations.

The term "legal rule" is supposed to designate one or more sentences embracing the whole meaning of a legal rule as an entity. This means that one should require that the rule expressing the legal consequences of a hypothetically stated fact should state, besides many procedural prescriptions, the jurisdiction of the agencies which are (if necessary) to determine the factual situation and make the legal consequences concrete. Unfortunately, this requirement is a source of further misunderstanding. According to such a requirement, what are generally

[42] Kelsen ("The Function of the Pure Theory of Law," *Law, A Century of Progress* [New York, 1937], II, 231) translates the expression "the law," as many authors have done, with the French "droit."

[43] John Stuart Mill in his essay on Utilitarianism (*Utilitarianism, Liberty, and Representative Government,* p. 43) explains that the German word Recht is "synonymous with law."

[44] Although "Gesetz" is often translated by the word "law."

called legal rules are only rule fragments. The so-called legal principles may be regarded as fragments pertaining to a greater number of legal rules.

Professor Roscoe Pound, recognizing that the term "law" has many meanings, which he reduced to three in his analysis, proposed "to unify them by the idea of social control—social control by a regime operating through a judicial and an administrative process carried on in accordance with a body of authoritative precepts and an authoritative technique."[45] We know that the *types* of legal rules are only rarely analyzed.[46]

The term "legal rule" implies the heteronomy of a rule. Heteronomous rules can be contrasted with autonomous rules. Popularly expressed, nobody can set legal rules for himself.[47] In the case The City of London *vs.* Wood (1701), Chief Justice Holt[48] pointed out this principle in a straightforward, simple manner. The concept of obedience in a legal sense is given by the heteronomous character of the legal rule. Max Weber's classical definition of the

[45] *Contemporary Juristic Theory*, pp. 16-17.

[46] With reference to the so-called written law, cf. Ernst Freund, *op. cit.*, pp. 53 ff.; Blachly-Oatman, "Federal Statutory Administrative Orders," 25 *Iowa Law Rev.* 582 ff.

[47] Jason de Mayno (*Comm. to Dig.*, I, 4, 1) asserted at the end of the fifteenth century that the Prince and the Pope can do whatever they want to do: "supra jus, et contra jus, et extra jus."—Quoted from A. T. Carlyle, "Conception médiévale du droit," *Report, 1937-38*, pp. 25-26.

[48] 12 Mod. 669, quoted in R. K. Gooch, *Source Book on the Government of England* (New York, 1939), p. 110.

conception of obedience also elucidates the concept of the heteronomy of a rule. "'Obedience' should mean: that the obedient person behaves essentially as if he had made the content of the command the maxim of his conduct for the command's sake, and so acts *exclusively* by the formal reason of the obedience-relationship, without regard to his personal judgment based on the grounds of the value or unworthiness of the command."[49]

There are limitations to the heteronomy of the legal rule when applied to the behavior of the constituent authority of a state and the rules set by this agency. Such rules may be regarded, as far as they determine the jurisdiction of the supreme authority, as autonomous in the legal sense.[50] The principle of heteronomy is not opposed to a fixed jurisdiction enabling agencies to *create* the rules by which the agency is to operate in the future and which also bind the agency itself until repealed or otherwise expressly limited.[51] The principle of heteronomy is not even opposed to allowing the agency to decide according to its own discretion (i.e., to choose among virtually equivalent conceptions), for the determined jurisdiction directs it to choose according to its discretion. That is why the term "discretion" has in a legal system the sense of a *directed* choice. The

[49] *Wirtschaft und Gesellschaft* (Tübingen, 1922), p. 123.
[50] See Hobbes, *Leviathan,* Part II, Chap. 26 [138].
[51] See A. S. Beardsley, *Legal Bibliography and the Use of Law Books* (Chicago, 1937), pp. 78 f.

creation of an individual decision entails another directed choice by the agency's having to determine (in a certain sense artificially) the factual situation[52] on which the decision is based.

Our experience shows that the means influencing human social conduct (including a particular technique) and the institutions which are created are in some regards similar in the process of time and among many nations; in other regards they are entirely different. Commonly adopted denominations often deceive us into believing that means and institutions with the same name are similar because their denomination is the same.

Eugen Ehrlich in a posthumous study discussed the question whether or not there is "such a thing as a world-wide Law." He answered in the affirmative with reference to all civilized peoples and civilized states and stated that, even with uncivilized and half-civilized peoples, "the whole scheme will hardly be absent."[53] The article was published in 1922. Professor Ehrlich assumed that with reference to the new Russia, "In some respects an exception is constituted."[54] He emphasized that frequently

[52] The restrictions in using illegally obtained evidence are significant for the statement that the legal truth may deviate from the historical truth. Cf. cases cited in 34 *Ill. Law Rev.* 758-62 (1940).

[53] "The Sociology of Law," 36 *Harv. Law Rev.* 131. Cf. Sir Paul Vinogradoff, *Introduction to Historical Jurisprudence*, Introduction (London, 1920), pp. 153-55, and Timasheff, *op. cit.*, pp. 70 ff.

[54] "The Sociology of Law," 36 *Harv. Law Rev.* 131. Carl Schmitt (*Verfassungslehre* [München, 1928], pp. 138-39) discusses the specific properties of a legal rule (Rechtsnorm), differentiating it from

"where diametrically opposed views are expressed, so here too affirmation and negation rest upon the use of similar words to designate different things with the result that the opposing parties talk past each other."[55]

Because of the present political evolution, it may come about that in using legal and political terms one will have to designate the political doctrine according to which the term is used. We know it is true that in a more or less extensive territory all other rule systems may become subordinated to a united rule system of human conduct subjecting all human activities (and by means of propaganda even the thinking of men) to one despotic agency commanding the usage of traditional legal terms. In such systems the whole sphere of human living may be declared as "social" conduct, and the individual may come to be a cell of a specific social order scarcely surpassed in subordination by the ants and bees.[56] I suppose that the concept of legal rules of such communities has to be distinguished from legal rules as conceived in the traditional manner.

an arbitrary command of a dictator. Schmitt registered the opinions of Alexejev, Timasheff, and Mirkine-Guetzevitch, who do not regard the rules of human conduct enforceable in Russia as legal rules. Cf. John Dickinson, *Administrative Justice and the Supremacy of Law in the United States* (Cambridge, 1927), pp. 120 f.

[55] "The Sociology of Law," 36 *Harv. Law Rev.* 131.

[56] "The wonder has always been," writes W. M. Wheeler, "not that there are so many differences in structure between such disparate organisms as insects and men, but that there are so many striking similarities in behavior."—*Social Life among Insects* (New York, 1923), p. 18.

II

LEGAL RULES AS PARTS OF A LEGAL SYSTEM

LEGAL SYSTEMS relate to the *highest* form of social organization called the state. Each legal system belongs to a state.[1] I shall not discuss here the question whether the rules relating to the Catholic Church or to interstate organizations[2] are generally called legal rules,[3] or whether or not the concept of supranational or international legal rules and the concept of "law-making agreements"[4] is consistent with the concept of national legal systems. The legal character of rules of human social conduct has often been evaluated in international law with reference to the nonexistence of regular law-enforcing agencies.[5] Lawrence in defining international law deliberately avoids using the word "law."[6]

[1] Ferdinand Lassalle discussed in his essay "About Constitutions" what would happen if in a modern state the legal system should cease to work. —*Collected Speeches and Writings*, ed. by Eduard Bernstein (Berlin, 1919), II, 25 ff.

[2] See H. Lauterpacht, *op. cit.*, pp. 431 f.

[3] Cf. the theory of nonjuristic issues of D. Schindler, "Schiedsgerichtsbarkeit und Friedenswahrung," *Festgabe für Fleiner* (Zürich, 1937), p. 13; and Lauterpacht, *op. cit.*, pp. 144, 157 f.

[4] Lauterpacht, *op. cit.*, pp. 415-16.   [5] *Ibid.*, p. 423.

[6] T. J. Lawrence, *The Principles of International Law* (London, 1929), p. 2.

It is often stated that the concept of a self-centered state today implies the presence of a "legal" system. This would mean that every state is in this particular sense a "legal" one, and this would lead to the conclusion that the expression "legal state" is a pleonasm. Since many writers have expressed this view, we shall have to discuss the foundations of such an assumption.

To be sure, under certain conditions, which are often called revolution, invasion, etc., some of the requirements for a legal system may not be fulfilled. That is why such circumstances may cause a status of *vacuum juris,* without having to be regarded as a vacuum with reference to rules of human social behavior. Even in such times there are certain rules complied with and enforced; but there is no legal system, and there are no legal rules in the common sense of the expression. If the rules are called legal rules their concept is not identical with the concept of legal rules as used in this paper. An invasion may be conceived of as the temporary incorporation of a rule system into the legal rule system of the invading country. I assume that there is no common understanding concerning these questions. Perhaps, after the present European war, new political and legal categories will arise which will cover these situations.[6a]

[6a] See *Military Government* (Basic Field Manual, Washington, Government Printing Office, 1940), *passim.*

Sir Paul Vinogradoff in his *Outlines of Historical Jurisprudence* accentuated not only the interdependence between state and law but regarded it as impossible "to think of a State without law."[7] However, Vinogradoff recognized that the state ought to be not only an "embodiment of power" but also assumed that a "juridical arrangement" is required too. He pointed to the "cynical conclusions" of "modern worshippers of brute force like Gumplowicz."[8] In his paper *Custom and Right* it is found that "the existence of legal orders involves delimitation and restriction of the wills and powers of members of the community, including in highest stages of civilization the government itself."[9] Hans Kelsen in many of his works asserted that the idea of a "legal" state should be regarded as using more words than necessary, for he held that no state was without a legal system and considered the concept of "law" and "state" from this particular point of view as identical.[10] This identification of law and state has been the main reason that Professor Kelsen, one of the fighters for democratic forms of government, has been attacked as justifying and legalizing absolutistic political doctrines.[11] Tima-

[7] (London, 1920), I, 84.   [8] *Ibid.*, pp. 86-87.
[9] (Oslo, H. Ascheboug & Co., 1925), p. 9.
[10] See, for example, *Der soziologische und der juristische Staatsbegriff* (Tübingen, 1928), *passim*. For the opinions of Somlo and Radbruch, see *ibid.*, pp. 202 f.
[11] Eric Voegelin, discussing one of the main works of Kelsen (*Allgemeine Staatslehre* [Berlin, 1925]), stressed that Kelsen had the

sheff does not recognize a despotic structure as a
legal state because, under despotic rule, the ruler
himself is not bound by his rules. He regards
Stammler's pertinent distinction as the best. To be
sure, Stammler discussed this distinction as mentioned by Timasheff many times. However, we
should recall Stammler's words, "Despotism means
still a legal situation,"[12] and assuming that, even in
a despotism, there are many other social forces in
operation, he teaches, "Though such a despotism
represents a very miserable social *situation,* as a
whole, however, it constitutes a *legal* order."[13]

Professor Stammler was not too clairvoyant when
he assumed that so "naked a despotism does not appear in our age."[14] (The second edition of his legal
philosophy was published in 1928.) I do not think
that the distinctive point mentioned by Stammler
and Timasheff is the most significant for the differentiation of a despotic from a legal state. A despotic
ruler may consider the rules, though despotic as to

chance "to put his theories into practice . . . drafting the Austrian
Constitution in accordance with his principles." Indeed, this constitution may be regarded as an embodiment of the democratic political
doctrine. Voegelin finishes his study emphasizing that "The pure
theory of law thus signifies not only an important progress in legal
analysis and technique, but also a development from the half-absolu-
tistic philosophy of the German Empire toward the spirit of the new
democracy."—"Kelsen's Pure Theory of Law," 42 *Pol. Sc. Quar.* 276.
See J. L. Kunz, *op. cit.,* p. 371.

[12] *Lehrbuch der Rechtsphilosophie* (Berlin, 1928), p. 93. Cf. Rudolf von Ihering, *Law as a Means to an End,* trans. by I. Husik
(New York, 1924), p. 253.

[13] *Rechtsphilosophie,* p. 94.   [14] *Ibid.,* p. 93.

content, as binding on himself. It is rather significant that states calling themselves totalitarian very
definitely reject the idea of being despotic. The
Italian doctrine (which in official publications assumes that "The totalitarian state is democratic, for
it is including of all. . . .") defines despotism as "a
government of one in the interests of one."[15] Thus
it adopts the characteristics of despotism as evolved
by the Greek philosophers, Thomas Aquinas, and
Kant.

Obviously the discussion of this matter is a two-
fold one. On the one hand, many people do not call
a despotic rule system a legal one,[16] while other
people do. On the other hand, many scholars attach
political consequences to this discussion. Timasheff,
for instance, wrote that "If State and Law are the
same thing looked at from different points of view,
then the historical struggle of European nations to
endow their political life with the principle of legality lacked meaning and sense. For according to
the theory discussed, there is no fundamental difference between the rule of the Stuarts and parliamentary government."[17] I feel sure that the contrary

[15] Official Guide of Ministry of Popular Culture, quoted in *Fascist
Era, Year XVII* (Rome, 1939), pp. 23-24.

[16] There are—as here discussed—different views on the elements
which divide a legal system from a despotic one. We have to realize
that the characterizations despotic, dictatorial, totalitarian, etc., are far
from fully descriptive. Charles Edward Merriam uses for the new
political systems the term "new despotism."—*The New Democracy
and the New Despotism* (New York, 1939), pp. 217 ff.

[17] *Op. cit.,* pp. 216-17.

doctrines put the despotic and the legal states in one category only from a legal point of view ("legal" as conceived by them). For these scholars (whose proposition I do not adopt) the difference between the rule of the Stuarts and parliamentary government is a *political* and not a legal one. It is not out of place to quote in this connection Blackstone's discussion of the jurisdiction of the British Parliament. Blackstone, adopting Sir Edward Coke's view that the power of the British Parliament is "transcendent and absolute," assumed that this Parliament is "the place where that absolute despotic power, which must in all governments reside somewhere, is intrusted by the constitution of these kingdoms." And further: "It can, in short, do every thing that is not naturally impossible. . . . True it is, that what the parliament doth, no authority upon the earth can undoe. . . ." Blackstone, opposing Locke, refused to discuss from a legal standpoint revolutionary acts against a despotic government which abuses the trust conferred upon it.[18] Karl Wolff some years ago wrote that a rule making it obligatory to kill women giving birth to twins is regarded by him as law from the point of view of legal science, although such a rule is not right from the point of view of morals.[19]

[18] I Comm. 160-61.

[19] "Der Rechtsbegriff," *Recueil Gény*, I, 188. (The contraction *Recueil Gény* is here used for: *Recueil d'études sur les sources du droit en l'honneur de François Gény*, Paris, Recueil Sirey, year of publication not indicated.) C. E. Merriam, discussing the opinions of Hegel, Austin and Dicey, writes: "Practically such commands may not

May I indicate some points in connection with those elements of a legal system, as discussed in this paper, which seem to be characteristic of modern despotic forms of government? The individual is not dealt with as a social, economic, and political entity.[20] That is why he cannot effectively examine whether or not a rule of his conduct and an authority which pretends to be a public agency corresponds to the main organizing rules—if any— of the supposedly legal order. The individual is regarded merely as a cell which must blindly obey orders of authorities with an unlimited or indeterminate jurisdiction. There is no social machine which is endowed with independence for determining the legality of specific decisions. The despotic regime, being totalitarian and exclusive, tends to embrace all human activities (even thinking). The formulation and manifestation of rules is not regarded as a prerequisite of their existence. The general knowability of rules of conduct is rather limited. Ex post facto laws are very frequent. There is a system of coercive realities, but there is no *rule system* in a despotic state, as it is conceived with the concept of a *legal* order, for the main organizing principles of the state (constitution) are either embalmed in hazy

be obeyed, but legally, in the narrower and stricter sense, they cannot lawfully be opposed."—*The Role of Politics in Social Change* (New York, 1936), p. 30.

[20] The recognition of the individual as an entity is accentuated in connection with all concepts of law by Vladimir Gsovski.—"The Soviet Concept of Law," 7 *Fordh. Law Rev.* 2.

principles of a social doctrine or, if manifested in a published constitution, they are not taken seriously.[21] It should be noted that even the dogma of infallibility of the Pope as determined by the Vatican Council (July 18, 1870) has been limited in substance and in form. It applies to the doctrine "on faith and morals" and to propositions expressed (formulated) by the Pope "when he speaks ex cathedra." The points here emphasized will become clearer in the following pages.

A legal rule can be conceived only in the network of a legal *system* with other legal rules. However, several eminent European scholars have assumed that a legal *system* can consist of only a single unwritten rule, vesting in one man the whole power over human social conduct without time limitation and without his even being bound by his previous acts and promises.[22] Nevertheless, I believe that the concept of a legal system implies a large number of

[21] See, for instance, Art. 125 of the Constitution of the Union of Soviet Socialist Republics guaranteeing freedom of speech, freedom of the press, freedom of assembly and meetings, and freedom of street processions and demonstrations. Vladimir Gsovski finishes his study "The Soviet Concept of Law" (7 *Fordh. Law Rev.* 43) with the sentence: "The Soviet statute is now the law in the eyes of soviet jurists, but this law is devoid of the basic concept of rights."

[22] Cf. Laun, "Eine Theorie vom möglichen Recht," *Archiv des öffentlichen Rechts, 1913,* p. 389; Kelsen, *Das Problem der Souveränität* (Tübingen, 1920), p. 97; and Weyr (criticizing a paper of Pitamic) in *Archiv des öffentlichen Rechts, 1916,* p. 345. Rudolf Stammler (*Rechtsphilosophie,* p. 93) expressed this principle with some limitations. Karl Loewenstein discusses the differences "between monarchy and one-man dictatorial rule" in a recent study, "The Demise of the French Constitution of 1875," 34 *Amer. Pol. Sc. Rev.* 882 ff.

legal rules.   F. Somlo[23] was right in emphasizing that legal rules are a *multum tantum*.

It may be interesting to mention that, as early as 1921, Carl Schmitt[24] characterized the dictator as a person who "may provide all necessary arrangements required by the factual situation. Legal questions are not to be considered in such a case, since only the appropriate implements for the particular end are important."   And further: "The dictator is interested, not in law, but in the proper functioning of the state, that is, the mere enforcement of his will, not subjecting the executive power to preceding legal rules."

The teaching of Carl Schmitt that dictators do not care whether or not their actions are regarded (or called) as "legal," does not always correspond to

[23] *Op. cit.*, p. 97. Edgar Bodenheimer (*op. cit.*, pp. 14, 25) expressed the same idea in another way.

[24] See *Die Diktatur* (München, 1921), p. 11. Whether such systems should be regarded as legal is answered by Mr. Justice Miller in Loan Association *vs.* Topeka, 20 Wall. 655 (1875): "There are limitations of such powers, which arise out of the essential nature of all free governments; implied reservations of individual rights, without which the social compact could not exist and which are respected by all governments entitled to the name." The same idea was expressed by Euripides through Theseus ("The Suppliants," *The Plays of Euripides in English* [London, Dent], II vd., p. 296): "Where no laws exist which bind the whole community, and one man rules, upon his arbitrary will alone depend the laws; and all thy rights are lost." Montesquieu (*The Spirit of Laws*, Book VI, Chap. 3) writes: "In despotic governments, there are no laws, the judge himself is his own rule." Professor Roscoe Pound (*Contemporary Juristic Theory*, p. 35) assumed that "Controversy over whether there is anything more than power and force behind social control by politically organized society is nothing new." See Roscoe Pound (*ibid.*, p. 18) about systems which do not require law or laws.

actual situations. We know that dictators have
made and often do make great efforts to maintain
formalities in order to have their actions called
"legal." Obviously dictators have been excellent
psychologists and, as such, they have been aware of
the peculiar suggestive influence which seems to be
attached to the terms "legal" and "lawful."[25] However, their concept of legality has greatly differed
from the concept of this term as used in countries
governed according to other than dictatorial principles. "The old idea that words possess magical
powers is false; but its falsity is the distortion of a
very important truth," writes Aldous Huxley.[26]

The concept that legal rules must necessarily be
connected in a rule system implies several points
with reference to the relationship between a particular legal rule and the rule system to which it belongs. Each legal rule is hallmarked by the system
of which it is a part. A legal rule must contain
directly or indirectly all the elements of what is

[25] According to Timasheff (*op. cit.*, p. 254), "The words 'law,'
'statute,' 'court,' and a thousand others have gradually become stimuli
of submission." A newer (modified) opinion of Carl Schmitt is contained in his statement quoted by Karl Loewenstein, "Law in the
Third Reich," 45 *Yale Law Rev.* 813, footnote 121. With reference
to the tendency to make the actions of totalitarian regimes be regarded
as "legal," see Alfred von Wegerer, "The Origins of this War: A German View," 18 *Foreign Affairs* 700 ff. Italy has been called in recent
official publications a *constitutional* monarchy. Cf. the opinion of C. F.
Merriam in *Political Power* (New York, 1934), pp. 12-13. Karl Loewenstein describes with what extreme sense for legality the French Constitution of 1875 was destroyed in June, 1940.—"The Demise of the
French Constitution," 34 *Amer. Pol. Sc. Rev.* 894.

[26] *Words and Their Meanings* (Los Angeles, 1940), p. 8.

called a legal system as a whole, and additional elements determined by the particular legal system for the rules belonging to it. The legal system is regarded as a higher unit composed of lower entities: legal rules. Common usage and science often differentiate between such higher and lower units.[27] The higher unit with reference to its parts is called "the whole" (in German called Ganzheit and sometimes, in a physical sense, Gestalt). Legal rules can be conceived *only* as *parts* of *their* "whole." The adjective "legal" implies this meaning. A legal rule created by a municipality can be conceived as a legal rule only in connection with its legal system as a whole; it cannot even be conceived as segregated from the constitution of the state and from other rules enabling the municipality to create legal rules. Legal rules are regarded (in a figurative sense) as part of a *living* rule organism.

Philosophy has always been concerned with the relationship between the whole and its parts, between the organic and the inorganic, the human body and its cells, the melody and the single tone, and so on. It has often been questioned whether the whole is "only" the mere sum of its parts and whether the properties of the whole are only the sum of the properties of its parts, or whether the whole acquires new properties in addition to those of its

[27] See Aristotle, *Metaphysics,* 1023 b, 1024 a, and Edmund Husserl, *Logische Untersuchungen* (Halle a. d. S., 1928), II, Part I, 225-88.

parts. It is certain that common usage distinguishes between the meaning of "the sum" and "the whole." The question arises, too, whether the lower unit (the part) acquires new properties as a result of its connection with other units in the whole. The problem becomes even more involved by the assertion that the higher unit retains its identity (according to the common usage) even if certain of its parts are changed. The human body, many social units, vegetables, and so on are commonly regarded as identical, or stable, despite the fact that we have evidence that the parts of these organisms are constantly being changed in the process of time. Likewise, a legal order is regarded as identical in spite of the fact that we are aware that some of its parts (the legal rules) are gradually eliminated and replaced by others.[28] One of the main difficulties in this reasoning may be removed when we recall that common usage applies the term "identical" and "identity" in cases

[28] Professor Felix Kaufmann ("The Significance of Methodology for the Social Sciences," 5 *Social Research* 463) formulated the term of "half-rigid" rules, where "in the very hierarchy of rules there is a provision for changes of rules. . . . In the very order of law are contained the principles for changes in the law." According to A. N. Whitehead (*Science and the Modern World* [London, Pelican, 1938], p. 233), only "The low type of organisms have achieved a self-identity dominating their whole physical life. Electrons, molecules, crystals, belong to this type." John Wild ("The Concept of the Given in Contemporary Philosophy—Its Origin and Limitations," 1 *Philosophy and Phenomenological Research* 81) writes: "Change certainly involves more than such a succession of discontinuous entities, namely, the persistence of something which endures throughout the change as a substance or substratum, binding the distinct phases into one continuous process."

where certain *main* features of the system and its traditional and specific technique remain seemingly unchanged. Mr. Justice Cardozo taught: "The law has its formulas, and its methods appropriate to conservation, and its methods and formulas appropriate to change."[29]

The legal system may be regarded from the *legal* point of view as composed of legal rules only. However, such statements are instructive only from a didactic point of view. They are instructive in expressing the proposition that all legal rules, general and individual, are based on the constitution and on other principles, rules, or facts *only* on the condition that these determining facts are recognized as relevant by the legal order itself. We know by experience that the legal order does not determine human social conduct solely by legal rules directly. It creates by legal rules institutions and provisions for determining or influencing human social conduct indirectly. The working of modern parliaments[30] and modern public administration furnishes many examples for this statement.

Jurisprudence distinguishes between two kinds of rules pertaining to a legal system. One kind is: the abstract expression of the direct or indirect legal consequences of one or several hypothetically stated

[29] *The Paradoxes of Legal Science* (New York, 1930), p. 8.

[30] The establishment and the function of investigating committees, whose formal jurisdiction consists of mere fact finding, often indirectly but vigorously influence human social conduct.

possible situations without relating it immediately to
certain persons or to an exactly determined factual
situation. Such rules are broadly called general
(abstract) legal rules or rules of general applicability. When people adapt their conduct to the ab-
stractly prescribed manner of conduct, the aim of
the legal rule is regarded as attained.[31] Not all
general rules directly express the legal consequences
of certain factual situations so that people can adapt
their conduct *immediately* to the rule. Rules establishing the jurisdiction (or discretion) of an agency
may be regarded as examples. Whether the fixing
of discretionary powers (which is identical with a
determination of jurisdiction) should be regarded
as limits of free (arbitrary) action or as a standard
according to which agencies have to act is an idle
question. From the point of view of *general* jurisprudence it seems idle to classify agencies according
to the forms of discretion conferred upon them.

The chief characteristic of individual rules (or
specific decisions) is: the expression of the legal consequences of one of several factual situations with
reference to a particular person or group of persons.[32]
Sometimes the boundaries of general rules and
specific decisions merge. The decision of a court

[31] "Indeed, if we muster even an imaginary statistical survey of
the facts of everyday life, we shall find that a rule of conduct is
kept a thousandfold for every breach of it."—B. Malinowski, Introduction to H. Jan Hogbin, *Law and Order in Polynesia,* pp. lxx-lxxi.

[32] Edmund Husserl's distinction between general and individual
truths may be applied here also.—*Logische Untersuchungen,* I, 231.

relating to the taxing power of a municipality is an individual decision for the municipality, but it is a general rule for the citizens who are paying the taxes. A rule determining the jurisdiction of a certain person, or expressing his duty to create a more concrete general rule, may be regarded as an individual rule relating to one person, but a general rule in relation to other persons. Even the assumption that a specific decision must relate to a certain *person* or *persons* is not entirely distinctive. It may relate to other concrete circumstances which make it specific or individual in contrast to general (abstract) rules. Although there is a fairly general understanding as to what general rules and individual decisions are, it must be emphasized that there is no sharp line of demarcation between general and specific.[33] With considerable exaggeration it may be stated that a general rule should be reducible to a definite number of specific rules.

In a complicated legal order certain agencies have jurisdiction to regularly create general rules.[34] The

[33] See Ernst Freund, *op. cit.*, pp. 28 ff. Sec. 1, Par. 1 of the British *Emergency Powers (Defence) Act, 1939* may be regarded, in relation to the British Crown, as an individual rule, whereas, in relation to the ordinary citizens, as a general rule. This provision reads: "Subject to the provisions of this section, His Majesty may by Order in Council make such Regulations . . . as appear to him to be necessary or expedient for securing the public safety, the defence of the realm, the maintenance of public order and the efficient prosecution of any war in which His Majesty may be engaged, and for maintaining supplies and services essential to the life of the community."

[34] With reference to American state constitutions, see Harvey Walker, *Law Making in the United States* (New York, 1934), pp. 258 f.

creation of such general rules is sometimes called a legislative or sublegislative function; the creation of individual decisions is denoted differently—when controversies are decided it is often called adjudication. Although legislative agencies usually create only general rules, they may create individual rules as well.[35] Although adjudicating agencies usually create only individual decisions, they may have jurisdiction to create general rules. It should be emphasized again that in the prevailing majority of cases general rules are complied with by people without individual decisions being rendered by public agencies.[36] It is presumed from a *legal point of view* that people comply with general rules in order to

[35] Cf. Robert Luce, *Legislative Problems* (Boston, 1935), pp. 572 ff.; Lotz, *Das Individualgesetz nach deutschem Reichsrecht* (Berlin, 1933), pp. 1 ff. Art. 7 of the ordinance of the Italian King, September 24, 1931, provides that ordinances relating only to particular persons do not have to be published in the Official Bulletin.—*Disposizioni riguardanti la promulgazione e pubblicazione delle leggi e dei decreti* (Rome, 1932), p. 8.

[36] Sir John Salmond (*Jurisprudence* [London, 1924], p. 57) connects the concept of law with the concept of courts: "No rule that is not thus in fact observed in accordance with the established practice of the courts is a rule of law, and conversely, every rule that is thus in fact observed amounts to a rule of law." As explained later on, I suppose that the opinion of Sir John Salmond does not correspond to reality. Thus, I am sure that people will generally comply with the Selective Training and Service Act of 1940 and with the Proclamation and other pertinent executive orders of the President of the United States. People will regard these rules as *legal,* although there is no established practice of the courts with reference to them. People will presume that these rules are legal, so long as the courts do not reverse this judgment, just as a reversing judgment, if made, will be regarded as existent, despite the possibility that the courts may later change their opinion.

avoid unfavorable legal consequences which may follow noncompliance with the legal rule. Noncomplying with a legal rule may mean that people are interpreting a legal rule with reference to a certain factual situation in another way from that in which the law-enforcing agency would interpret it. That is why people often try to interpret rules according to specific predictions. These predictions relate to a *hypothetical* evaluation of a factual situation by law-enforcing agencies with reference to a certain pre-existing legal rule, which may be a mere juris-diction-determining rule too.

The conventional denomination of a decision as a "specific" (individual) rule does not mean that it does not more or less concern other people living in the social community. The very fact that an individual decision can only be conceived of as a part of a legal system implies that this specific decision has to be complied with (in a particular sense recognized as binding) by everybody to whom the legal system relates. In this sense an individual decision is "general" too. From this point of view it can be assumed that generality is implied by all legal rules.[37]

The distinction between general and individual rules is significant, because several scholars call only

[37] Timasheff (*op. cit.,* p. 78) writes that "every ethical rule is combined with the idea of acting in conformity with it, is the duty not of one person, but of every person whom it concerns." That is why "The formula is always a general one. . . ."

general rules legal rules or laws;[38] others, only individual decisions.[39] Many of them suppose that only individual decisions have reality as legal rules because individual decisions determine the legal consequences with reference to a fixed factual situation. They regard general legal rules as propositions or as hints addressed to the law-enforcing agencies in order to give them a help in the creation of decisions.[40]

The concept of the legal rule as a general rule has often been connected with the political idea that all people are equally subject to a legal regulation.[41] This is especially emphasized by Gustav Radbruch,

[38] Cf. Sir Frederick Pollock, *A First Book of Jurisprudence* (London, 1923), p. 15; A. Brecht, "The Search for Absolutes," 7 *Social Research* 212 f.

[39] Professor John Chipman Gray wrote: "The law of a community consists of general rules which are followed by its judicial department in establishing legal rights and duties."—*Nature and Sources of the Law* (New York, 1927), p. 1.

[40] Jerome Frank ("Are Judges Human?" 80 *Penna. Law Rev.* 47) writes: "The legal rules unquestionably have some effect on an honest judge while he is making up his mind how to decide a 'contested' case. . . . Thus it is specific, enforceable decisions (judgments, orders and decrees) which determine all legal rights and duties. Enforceable decisions, not legal rules. . . ." The expression "legal rule" is used by Frank in another sense from that in which I am using it, but the difference of opinion is obvious.

[41] Cf. Carl Schmitt, *Politische Theologie* (München, 1934), p. 19; E. Bodenheimer, *op. cit.*, p. 27. John Dickinson ("A Working Theory of Sovereignty," 42 *Pol. Sc. Quar.* 525) writes: "A system of law purports to be a body of general rules which produce like decisions in like cases. . . ." Rudolf von Ihering (*op. cit.*, p. 253) divides the "legal imperatives of the state" into concrete and abstract. He calls only the abstract legal imperatives "legal norms."

who does not recognize individual decisions as legal rules.[42]

Insofar as the question of terminology is concerned, I suppose that common usage designates both general and individual rules as legal rules.[43] This common denomination does not prevent the examination of the significance of both kinds of legal rules. It should be stressed that authors denying the legal-rule character of general rules often do not analyze the legal character of the rules which determine the jurisdiction of the individual rule-creating agency.

[42] "Le but du droit," published in the *Report, 1937-1938*, pp. 50, 52.

[43] See Somlo, *op. cit.*, pp. 64-65. Thomas Hobbes (*Leviathan*, Part II, Chap. 26), after defining what civil law is, writes: "For every man seeth, that some laws are addressed to all the Subjects in generall; some to particular provinces; some to particular vocations; and some to particular Men; and are therefore Lawes. . . ." Carré de Malberg ("Réflexions très simples sur l'objet de la science juridique," *Recueil Gény*, p. 194) calls both types legal rules.

III

LEGAL RULES MANIFESTED IN A
HUMAN LANGUAGE

LEGAL RULES are generally manifested in a human
language either by the spoken or written word.
Sometimes such rules may be expressed by non-
linguistic signs as well—facial expressions, pictures,
gestures, stop lights, etc.[1] These nonlinguistic signs
are generally regarded as substitutes for linguistic
signs. By human convention they may be easily
transposed[2] into sentences of a human language—
otherwise they cannot serve as "sign vehicles"[3] for
legal rules. Even tacitness may become such a sign,[4]

[1] Thomas Hobbes (*Leviathan*, Part II, Chap. 26) defines the civil
law as rules which the Commonwealth has commanded "by word,
writing or other sufficient sign of the will. . . ." Savigny designates
law as "embodied in language." Cf. Holland, *op. cit.*, p. 43. F. E.
Lumley (*Means of Social Control* [New York, 1925], p. 325) discusses "overt features" in which commands are given.

[2] "Every judgment, however, can be expressed in words, though
not every judgment need be so expressed or can readily be so."—B.
Bosanquet, *The Essentials of Logic* (London, 1895), pp. 81-82.

[3] The term "sign vehicle" is used by Charles W. Morris, *Foundations of the Theory of Signs* (Chicago, 1938), p. 3. Edmund Husserl
(*Logische Untersuchungen*, II, Part 2, 8-9) examines which sign
vehicles are able to carry a meaning.

[4] Cf. Reinach, *Die apriorischen Grundlagen des bürgerlichen Rechtes*,
repr. from *Jahrbuch für Philosophie und phenomenologische Forschung*
(Halle, 1913), I, 24-25; Stenzel, "Philosophie der Sprache," *Handbuch
der Philosophie* (München, 1934), IV, 105-6; and Hobbes, *The El-*

if pre-existing sign vehicles establish it as meaningful. The use of non-linguistic signs designating legal
rules or rule fragments is a mere technical problem.
"Nothing is intrinsically a sign or a sign vehicle but
becomes such only insofar as it permits something
to take account of something through its media-
tion," writes Charles W. Morris.[5] The legal rule has
necessarily spatial qualities embodied in its sign
vehicle. Even presuming that tacitness serves as a
sign vehicle, one has to learn whose tacitness, when,
where, and by whom observed, has given to it a
significant meaning. The assertion that a legal rule
exists always implies that some sign vehicle coexists
in union with it.

There is a considerable difference in expressing a
legal rule in a spoken and in a written form.[6] In
transforming an oral text into a written one it may
be difficult to control the accurate transfer of the
accent and the emphasis. On the other hand, in
transforming a written into an oral text, it is difficult to verify whether or not punctuation marks and

ements of Law Natural and Politic, Part I, Chap. XIII, Par. 11. Walter Jellinek (*Verwaltungsrecht* [Berlin, 1931], p. 270) discusses "tacit
acts of public administrative authorities." See, for example, Sec. 8a
of the Securities Act of 1933, which provides "that registration
statements [as amended] become effective 20 days after filing and
the registrant is then entitled to sell securities. Non-action is, thus,
in effect, tantamount to issuance of a license. . . ."—*Monograph No.
26, Securities and Exchange Commission* (The Attorney General's
Committee on Administrative Procedure, Washington, 1940), p. 305.

[5] *Op. cit.,* p. 45.

[6] See L. Bloomfield, *Linguistic Aspects of Science* (Chicago, 1939),
p. 6, and F. E. Lumley, *op. cit.,* pp. 325 f.

other signs (sometimes of decisive importance) have been correctly transcribed. These differences have always been disregarded in legal science. In present legal theory and practice, writing is assumed to mirror perfectly orally expressed rules, and both forms of manifestation are often interchanged. But although this interchange is arbitrary and not well founded, legal convention has tolerated this inexactitude.

The usual form of expressing and recording legal rules in advanced societies is in writing. It is generally recognized that this form is the best method of recording from the point of view of legal security. Certain legal situations require the oral manifestation of legal rules. Thus, in a riot, the police officer will orally command the people to disperse.

Euripides regarded the advantages of the knowability of law in the written form as a means of eliminating the disadvantages which poor people have in learning a legal rule.[7] Sir Henry Sumner Maine called attention also to the *social* and *political* influences of the fact that the legal rule is written.[8] Montesquieu emphasized the relationship between governmental systems and the kinds of manifestation of the law.[9]

---

[7] "But under written laws the poor and rich an equal justice find." —Theseus in "The Suppliants," by Euripides, quoted by W. A. Robson, *Civilization and the Growth of Law*, p. 72.

[8] *Ancient Law* (London, Humphrey Milford, 1939), pp. 17, 19.

[9] "In what Governments and in what cases the Judges ought to determine according to the express letter of the law," in *The Spirit of Laws*, Book VI (London, George Bell & Sons, 1900), I, 81.

The general theory of signs is now in its beginning,[10] although in earlier times many scholars stressed the importance of its systematic treatment. That is the reason that it is difficult to write about the matter from the point of view of legal science. Here I will only call attention to the fact that it is of immense political importance what kind of sign is used for the expression of a legal rule. The importance of these problems cannot be limited to the science of mere legal technique.

It is hotly discussed whether thoughts can be adequately conveyed in a human language.[11] Such doubts have also been frequently expressed relating to the manifestation of legal rules.[12] In this regard legal science and legal technique share the difficulties of other rule systems and other sciences, but perhaps with more far-reaching social consequences.[13] These difficulties will increase in proportion to the intricate forms of human social relations and will diminish with the development of the theory of signs and of legal technique. They will

[10] F. de Saussure, *Cours de linguistique générale* (Paris, 1931), p. 34. A brilliant treatment of the main points of the doctrine of expression and meaning may be found in Edmund Husserl, *Logische Untersuchungen*, II, Part 1, 23-105.

[11] C. W. Morris, *op. cit.*, p. 26. Bréal (*Essai de Sémantique* [Paris, 1924], p. 107) poses the question: "Pourquoi les mots sont disproportionnés aux choses?"

[12] Hobbes, *The Elements of Law*, Part I, Chap. XIII, p. 68. G. Tarde (*La Logique sociale* [Paris, F. Alcan, 1895], p. 254) saw the problem more optimistically.

[13] See Ernst Freund, *op. cit.*, pp. 161 ff.

diminish, as well, with a close scrutiny into the political reasons why inadequate sign vehicles expressing legal rules are used deliberately.

The expression of a legal rule by a sign vehicle implies always the *formulation* of a legal rule, for the sign vehicle is the spatial localization of the legal rule in and to the external world.[14] This point is often underestimated or deliberately misunderstood in legal and political science. It is often stated that a legal rule can exist without a sign vehicle at all,[15] or with an incomplete sign vehicle which does not mirror the whole meaning of the legal rule. In other words, the legal rule has been conceived as a subjective thing without co-ordinated and adequate objectivity, i.e., without such spatial sign as the meaning of it requires in order to become understandable for other people. It has sometimes been supposed that legal rules may exist in the human mind without an appearance in the external world, even at the very moment of their beginning. Their place—if any—in space has been located in the human mind, a place indeed not easily recognizable to the law-abiding citizen. One may question whether or not the carrying of such rules in the head implies their formulation in words, whether or not such

[14] John Chipman Gray (*op. cit.,* p. 94) discusses "the rules *laid down* by the courts." (My italics.) The spatial localization implies "sense-data" making the signs or the formulae recognizable.

[15] Bergbohm discussed, without deeper analysis, *nonformulated* law.—*Jurisprudenz und Rechtsphilosophie* (Leipzig, 1892), p. 52. Cf. Wenzel, *Der Begriff des Gesetzes* (Berlin, 1920), pp. 34-49.

rules can be stored in the human mind inarticulately. Indeed, it appears that a legal rule essentially has to be manifested by signs and has to be recognizable and verifiable in and to the external world.[16] There is a considerable tendency to make the verification of the rules of general application easy.[17] The legal order may limit the number and specifically designate the persons to whom *certain* legal rules have to be recognizable. However, it cannot exclude all persons (save the creator or carrier of the rule) from its knowability. The manifestation of the rule cannot be preceded by its existence; it has in the process of time either to precede or coincide with the birth of the legal rule. The thought content of the rule may be regarded as a prenatal fact conditioning the creation of the rule, but not as a legal rule in itself. Thus a legal rule is essentially an *inter*-subjective (social) act contrasting with both the *intra*-subjec-

[16] Karl Wolff (*op. cit.*, pp. 182 f.) assumes that the concept of the law (Rechtsbegriff) implies that what is called law has to be noticeable (anmerkbar). Joseph W. Bingham ("What is Law," 11 *Mich. Law Rev.* 109, footnote 29) wrote: "I use the phrase 'the law' in the sense of sequences of external facts and their concrete legal consequences through the concrete operation of governmental machinery." However, it should be emphasized that, whereas Professor Bingham stressed the necessity of external facts, he did not admit that these facts are rules.

[17] According to A. S. Beardsley (*Legal Bibliography*, p. 7), "The term 'repositories of the law' has been applied to those books of primary authority which include the books of statute law and the books of case law. These two classes of law books are frequently referred to as the repositories of the law, since what is to be regarded as 'law' for any given jurisdiction must necessarily be found in books of either of these classes."

tive acts (not yet expressed *in* the external world) and pure monologues (not yet expressed *to* the external world), which are expressed but not knowable to other persons. This assumption implies that legal rules have necessarily to be formulated in words of a human language, or there must be a possibility of formulating them in this manner. The expression "unformulated law" may be regarded in this sense as a contradiction in terms.[18]

The question of what unwritten law and customary law is has often been complicated by the problem of unformulated law.[19] Blackstone obviously recognized this difficulty, asking "How are these customs or maxims to be known?"[20]

[18] E. Bodenheimer refers several times to the tendency of totalitarian states not to manifest their "legal" rules. He regards "preciseness, rationality and stability" as the "most essential features" of law. —*Op. cit.*, p. 79. Dr. Bodenheimer—referring to Eugen Ehrlich— writes that "to a free society these rules are formulated as precisely and definitely as possible."—*Ibid.*, p. 80. However, Ehrlich made in this regard a distinction between "legal propositions" and "legal norms."—Ehrlich, *Fundamental Principles*, p. 38.

[19] H. Lauterpacht (*op. cit.*, p. 426) writes: "The fact that the source of law is in its creation external to those bound by it may both in primitive and in modern society be effectively concealed behind the phenomenon of customary law."

[20] Blackstone (I *Comm.* 69) divides "The municipal law of England, or the rule of civil conduct prescribed to the inhabitants of this Kingdom" into two kinds: "The *lex non scripta*, the unwritten or common law; and the *lex scripta*, the written or statute law." He divides the unwritten or common law into three kinds: "1. General customs; which are the universal rule of the whole kingdom, and form the common law, in its stricter and more usual signification. 2. Particular customs; which, for the most part affect only the inhabitants of particular districts. 3. Certain particular laws; which, by custom, are adopted and used by some particular courts, of pretty general and extensive jurisdiction." Blackstone poses the question,

I have the impression that the question of what unwritten law is represents something like a bad conscience on the part of many legal theorists, and is one of the crucial problems of legal and political science. A treatment of what unwritten law is often descends to a mere play of words. The expression "unwritten law" has been abused for more than two thousand years in order to explain or to conceal sundry gaps in legal and political science. This ill-use of the word was clearly recognized by Maine, who emphasized that "English case-law is sometimes spoken of as unwritten, and there are some English theorists who assure us that if a code of English jurisprudence were prepared we should be turning unwritten law into written—a conversion, as they insist, if not of doubtful policy, at all events of the greatest seriousness. Now, it is quite true that there was once a period at which the English common law might reasonably have been termed unwritten. The elder English judges did really pretend to a knowledge of rules, principles, and distinctions which were not entirely revealed to the bar and to the lay public. Whether all the law which they claimed to monopolize was really unwritten, is exceedingly questionable; but at all events, on the assumption that there was once a large mass of civil

"How are these customs or maxims to be known, and by whom is their validity to be determined? The answer is by the judges. . . . They are the depositories of law; the living oracles, who must decide in all cases of doubt. . . ."

and criminal rules known exclusively to the judges, it presently ceased to be unwritten law. As soon as the courts of Westminster Hall began to base their judgments on cases recorded, whether in the year books or elsewhere, the law which they administered became written law. . . . But at no stage of this process has it any characteristic which distinguishes it from written law. It is written case law, and only different from code law because it is written in a different way."[21] Maine's phrase, "written in a different way," may be understood to mean "manifested through another written sign vehicle." Maine did not recognize as law anything not formulated and manifested in a human language. He found that "case law" may represent—as mentioned before—a sign vehicle for rules of human conduct, but he clearly saw that there is no legal rule that is not carried by a sign vehicle.[22] The history of the expression "unwritten" in a legal sense is very instructive, and one should expect the results of the study of this history to exercise a therapeutic influ-

[21] *Op. cit.*, p. 11.

[22] F. A. Ogg (*European Governments and Politics* [New York, 1939], p. 325) teaches: ". . . it was always characteristic of the common law, as it is today, that much of it was simply carried in men's minds without being written down, at any rate in an orderly manner." B. A. Wortley regards "binding precedents" as *written* law (with reference to the British legal system), just as statutes and ordinances.—"La théorie des sources en droit privé positif de François Gény considerée dans son rapport avec la jurisprudence anglaise," *Recueil Gény*, II, 23.

ence too. I doubt whether it is wise to use this word[23] in legal science at all.

It is generally recognized that specific decisions may contain general rules of human conduct, although their grammatical form, according to common usage, expresses only a specific decision relating to certain persons, times, and circumstances.[24] Many legal systems deliberately use individual decisions as sign vehicles for general rules containing legal consequences of similar factual situations as adjudicated in the specific decision and binding people whom the specific decision does not concern. Dicey pictures judge-made law as consisting "of rules to be collected from the judgments of the courts."[25] Such general rules are rules *for* conduct, just as legal

[23] J. C. Gray (*op. cit.*, p. 161) recommends the discontinuance of the use of the terms "written" and "unwritten" law. Professor Ernst Freund (*op. cit.*, pp. 3, 12) explains the expression "unwritten" as contrasting with "regulatory" rules: "A just appreciation of the relation between written and unwritten law must be based upon the recognition of a distinction between two types of rules, the one declaratory, the other regulative in character" (p. 3). Freund (p. 13) fully recognizes that what he calls declaratory law (unwritten law) must be covered by the will of the legislature to supplement, in this form, "regulatory law."

[24] A. Kocourek (*op. cit.*, pp. 142-43) writes: "The great bulk of the legal rules of our system are to be extracted from reported cases where decisions are stated on past states of fact. These decisions clearly cannot impose duties on the parties to litigation to act in a given way concerning the matters in dispute, since these matters of conduct are now beyond control. The court can and does prescribe what duties are now due owing to past conduct, but the important thing is the rule for the conduct itself; that is to say, conduct of the kind which an adjudicated case presents."

[25] *Law and Public Opinion in England* (London, 1926), pp. 361-62.

rules essentially are rules *for* conduct and never rules *of* conduct.

Individual decisions which will carry general rules are not always invoked incidentally. In several countries they are invoked purposely as a result of "test cases." This is done not only by private persons, but also by public agencies. Even "illegalities" are sometimes committed to provoke "test cases."

Individual decisions are not the most inadequate form of sign vehicles for conveying the meaning of general rules. We know by experience that even common social behavior as expressed in various forms—manifested doctrine and the like—is also used to convey the meaning of legal rules. For instance, Article 38 of the statute of the Permanent Court of International Justice determines as sign vehicles for the rules which the international court will use as standards for their decisions, international custom, judicial decisions, and the teachings of publicists.[26]

Why do people not use the most appropriate form of sign vehicle in order to express a certain meaning? We cannot answer this question satisfactorily

[26] International custom has to be used as *evidence* for an existing rule. This may be understood as a sign vehicle, or as a means of the verification of a sign vehicle. Judicial decisions and the teachings of publicists are considered as subsidiary means which should be used when there are no general principles of law recognized by civilized nations and when there are no other rules cited in Art. 38 of the statute. A similar system is used in Art. 1 of the Swiss Civil Code, Art. 7 of the Austrian Civil Code, Art. 3 of the Japanese Statute of the Administration of Justice, etc., as discussed below.

because we cannot answer the more general question of why human social life is not organizable in a completely rational manner. The use of sign vehicles that are not the most appropriate technically is connected with the complicated ego-structure of the legislator and with other deep, underlying facts. For the same reasons, terms with a very broad meaning or fictions as forms of expression are often applied.[27]

The sign vehicle is appropriate for carrying a legal rule if experience shows that people find it uniformly significant for their social conduct. The discovery and the understanding of a sign vehicle (the recognition that it exists and of what it designates) may be facilitated by various devices.[28] One of the most significant examples of such a device is represented by the highly efficient work of the American Law Institute in restating the main part of the common law in America.

The significance of a sign vehicle is subject to

[27] See Rodney L. Mott, "Natural Rights and Legislative Vagueness," in *Recueil Gény*, III, 44 ff., and J. W. Hedemann, *Die Flucht in die Generalklauseln* (Berlin, 1933), *passim*. There is a great deal of literature about the problem of legal fictions. Whereas *Webster's Collegiate Dictionary* (5th ed.) explains the word "fiction" in connection with law as "An assumption of a possible thing as a fact," *The Concise Oxford Dictionary of Current English* (3rd ed.) writes that the word "fiction" as a legal term or as a term of politeness is used in expressing a "conventionally accepted falsehood."

[28] See A. S. Beardsley, *op. cit.*, pp. 224 ff. See Lord Bacon's propositions concerning ". . . the way to reduce and recompile the laws of England" in his *Law Tracts*, Chap. I. Lord Bacon very often discussed in this study problems pertaining to legal certainty and predictability.

change in the process of time. It is a platitude that the meaning of words and sentences constantly changes. People consciously or unconsciously take these changes into account. Whereas the sign vehicle of a legal rule may remain stable, the rule carried by the sign vehicle may change.[29] The changing of the meaning of a legal sign vehicle may in time come to transform it into its opposite. Legal (and especially political) doctrine may exercise and does exercise a mighty influence upon the legal system by unconsciously and consciously determining the meaning of sign vehicles. Thus, language is an important canal of interaction between public opinion and a legal system. Frequently the meaning of a legal rule is—in a figurative sense—determined by a kind of daily plebiscite of the people. Is there linguistic validity with reference to a certain meaning at a certain time? Experience shows a sign vehicle may have several meanings. However, social and legal life operates on the basis of a certain linguistic validity.[30] In literally billions of cases people uniformly understand what a legal rule means. In a civilized society particular agencies are in charge of deciding, in the case of controversies, which of several meanings of a legal rule applies. It is inter-

[29] With reference to the assumption of Karl N. Llewellyn, "The subject matter with which the lawyer deals is not words but their meanings," see Carl J. Friedrich, "Remarks on Llewellyn's View of Law, Official Behaviour and Political Science," 42 *Pol. Sc. Quar.* 420.

[30] A. S. Beardsley (*op. cit.*, pp. 290 f.) gives a bibliography of law dictionaries and "sources" of legal definitions.

esting to note that in France, where the Council of State has to determine, upon the request of public authorities or of private persons, in certain cases "the real sense of an obscure act of the public administration,"[31] recourse to interpretation is rather rare.[32] Decisions of public agencies in pertinent cases thus supplement linguistic validity. The necessity for such decisions is relatively rare because people generally interpret sign vehicles carrying rules in such a way that they do not conflict with each other or with the legal order.[33] This common understanding of legal rules is often underestimated. The meaning of the legal rule is decidedly influenced by the changes in sub-ordinate or co-ordinate

[31] Louis Rolland, *Précis de droit administratif*, p. 267.   [32] *Ibid.*
[33] Professor Kocourek (*op. cit.*, p. 144) writes: "But it must be remembered that duties are not always clearly ascertainable *in advance*. Very commonly, the answer to the question of whether a duty *exists* and the scope of it, can not be *reliably known* until the question is litigated." (My italics.) The fact that it is not *always* ascertainable how the courts would or will interpret a legal rule does not influence the very existence of the rule. The legislator enacting a legal rule does not envisage a specific (judicial) process to make a legal rule reliably knowable. H. Lauterpacht (*op. cit.*, p. 425) writes: ". . . only through final ascertainment by agencies other than the parties to the dispute can the law be rendered certain; it is not rendered so by the *ipso dixit* of an interested party. Such certainty is of the essence of law." In the great majority of cases people abide by law according to their *ipso dixit*. I doubt whether the relationship between a rule as interpreted by an interested party and as decided by an agency should be always designated as being less and more "certain." The specific decision transforms the pre-existing rule in many regards; the decision is more than the old "duty" in a more "certain" shape. For parties not involved in the controversy, the predictability of how the agency would act would be easier. In this respect the rule is more "certain."

legal rules of the same legal system. For instance, the enacting of the Fourteenth Amendment to the American Constitution changed the meaning of a great part of American legal rules. The changing of a procedural rule may change the meaning of a great many rules of substantive law. Naturally, as mentioned elsewhere in this paper, the sign vehicle of what is called a legal rule may be regarded in this sense only as a fragment which should be complemented by all rules pertaining to it.[34]

There are two main methods of interpreting legal rules if the legal order itself does not regulate this topic. One of them is the logico-grammatical, the other the historical. Both methods are *generally* applied; there is a traditional technique in legal thinking but there is no such thing as a specifically juridical interpretation. "This applies to a literary or an artistic work, as well as to a law, an international treaty or moral canon."[35]

Human language is used as a sign vehicle, expressing legal rules according to the grammar of the language. We cannot say that adherence to the rules of grammar is an essential requirement; we only know that legal rules are usually expressed in this form. By human convention, even word combinations which are not in accordance with the rules of

[34] See A. Kocourek, *op. cit.*, p. 145.
[35] H. Kelsen, *Legal Technique in International Law*, p. 12. Kelsen is right in stating that "the historical interpretation and the logico-grammatical interpretation are of equal value. . . ."—*Ibid.*, p. 12.

grammar can become meaningful. The grammar of a language distinguishes between two functions of sentences. One is the cognitive, the other, the expressive. By the cognitive function we mean asserting something which may be true or false. For instance, "The sun is shining." Rudolf Carnap[36] divides the expressive function "into expressions with pictorial, emotional, and volitional functions." Sentences determining human behavior exercise a volitional expressive function. It is true that often this expressive volitional function of sentences is not easily recognizable as such because it is expressed in the grammatical form of sentences which are generally used as sign vehicles for assertions. Carnap writes: ". . . the situation is not so readily apprehended when sentences expressing a command have the grammatical form of assertions."[37] However, as will be explained later on, a legal rule must necessarily contain the assertion concerning the data of its creation or recognition. This asserting portion does not belong to the legal rule in the logico-grammatical sense; it belongs to it in the legal sense.

The discussion concerning the problem of which type of sign vehicle is adequate for a legal order, or for its particular parts, concentrates in some

[36] "Logic," in *Factors Determining Human Behavior* (Harvard Tercentenary Publications, Cambridge, 1937), pp. 109 ff. Roscoe Pound (*Contemporary Juristic Theory*, p. 46) discusses "the experience formulated in the body of authoritative legal precepts."

[37] *Op. cit.*, p. 111.

countries on the question to what extent the common law system can be substituted for statutory law. It has been generally recognized that the common law in its ancient and new form composes a very efficient weapon in guaranteeing several elements of a legal system which characterize it in contrast to despotic rule systems. It is significant that Mr. Justice Cardozo, who gave as a judge and as a scholar great assistance and strength to the tendencies pursued by modern legal technique, wrote in this connection: "The truth is that many of us, bred in common law traditions, view statutes with a distrust which we may deplore, but not deny."[38]

[38] *The Paradoxes of Legal Science,* p. 9.

IV

SOME ELEMENTS OF THE CONCEPT
"LEGAL SYSTEM"

LEGAL RULES determine human social conduct.[1] In different political systems they embrace wider or narrower portions of human social conduct. The determination of the limits of the so-called "self-help" should be regarded as a regulation of social conduct as well. Some authors state that legal rules relate not only to human *conduct* or, as John Austin emphasized, to the *course* of human conduct,[2] but also to human *conviction,* that is, to intra-subjective conduct as well.[3] To be sure, legal rules may differentiate between different kinds of conduct which mirror various opinions or convictions, but I do not

[1] Mr. Justice Cardozo speaks of "the law as a guide of conduct. . . ."—*The Growth of the Law* (New Haven, 1934), p. 3. H. Kelsen ("The Function of the Pure Theory of Law," *Law, A Century of Progress,* II, 232) writes: "However one may define the essence of law, it cannot be denied that it constitutes a regulation of human behaviour." K. C. Allen (*Law in the Making* [Oxford, 1939], p. 1) determines as "sources of law," "those agencies by which rules of conduct acquire the character of law by becoming objectively definite, uniform, and, above all, compulsory." "All law is directed to conditions of things manifest to the senses."—O. W. Holmes, Jr., *The Common Law,* p. 49.

[2] *Op. cit.,* I, 98.

[3] Somlo, *op. cit.,* I, 69 f. Walter Jellinek (*Verwaltungsrecht,* p. 357) emphasizes that the public official is subject to "Gesinnungspflicht."

think that the subject matter of legal rules may be anything more than that which governs external human conduct.[4] Legal rules may be created with the political objective of influencing human conviction, for instance, relating to economic competition; but even such objectives do not change their subject matter. They may differentiate between the legal consequences of deliberate and accidental acts, but the subject matter of the regulation still relates to human conduct. They "can make an opinion (or a belief) obligatory, or more exactly they can force the subjects of law to take an attitude considered as the manifestation of a determined opinion (or belief)."[5] Justinian introduced his *Institutes* in this manner. Even such a regulation does not change the statement that legal rules determine human conduct and nothing else. T. E. Holland (referring to Aristotle and Kant) divides sciences into those dealing with "states of the will irrespectively of their

---

[4] Morris R. Cohen (*Law and the Social Order* [New York, 1933], p. 173) writes: "The subject matter of the law is the regulation of the conduct of individuals living on those more or less permanent relations which we call society." Georg Jellinek (*Allgemeine Staatslehre*, p. 333) opines that legal rules relate to the external conduct of man. K. N. Llewellyn (*The Bramble Bush, Some Lectures on Law and Its Study* [New York, 1930], p. 3) emphasizes: "It is much more common to approach the law as being *a set of rules of conduct,* and most thinkers would say rules of *external* conduct to distinguish them from the rules of morality. . . ." However, Llewellyn himself approaches law in another way.

[5] Kelsen, *Legal Technique in International Law*, p. 20. Section 9 of the British *Emergency Powers (Defence) Act, 1939* expressly recognized the British constitutional doctrine concerning "the powers exercisable by virtue of the *prerogative* of the Crown." (My italics.)

outward manifestation in act, and those which deal with states of the will only so far as they are manifested in action." The former science he calls Ethic, the latter, Nomology ("the conformity of actions to rules").[6]

A legal rule must expressively or by implication contain the link chaining it to the legal system during the whole time of its existence.[7] The grammatical sentence showing how the rule is associated with the legal system has the grammatical function of an assertion; that means that it can be true or false.[8] The assertion is made regularly by stating by whom, when, where the rule was created or recognized. The first constitution of a state establishing a legal system cannot and must not be linked with preceding legal rules. In this sense the first constitution must be regarded as a *political* fact. Such a political fact has to be conceived metajuridically.

A rule which is not linked to (covered by) a legal

[6] T. E. Holland, *op. cit.*, pp. 24-27.

[7] In this *particular sense* we have "to derive the laws prescribing what ought to be done from what is done." The much discussed proposition of Kant (*Critique of Pure Reason*, trans. by N. K. Smith [London, 1933], p. 313) reads: "for whereas, so far as nature is concerned, experience supplies the rules and is the source of truth, in respect to the moral laws it is, alas, the mother of illusion! Nothing is more reprehensible than to derive the laws prescribing what *ought to be done* from what is *done*, or to impose upon them limits by which the latter is circumscribed."

[8] I suppose that the here discussed assertive part of a legal rule has a broader meaning than "the character of being a decision" expressed in a statement, as H. Reichenbach puts it for so-called "logical facts." Cf. Reichenbach, *Experience and Prediction* (Chicago, 1938), pp. 11-12.

system cannot be regarded as a legal rule.[9] Both the disregarding of this principle and the tendency to apply it with a mechanical preciseness are sources of sterile discussions. Timasheff explained this interrelationship in a short but brilliant manner, discussing the objections concerning the discrepancy between abstract rules and judicial decisions. "Abstract legal rules are of course somewhat modified by courts and administrative bodies, but the relationship between abstract rules and concrete decisions is not that of discrepancy, but that of concretization. Writers who speak of discrepancy themselves involuntarily concretize the abstract rules in a broader manner than do the tribunals and then compare the two concretizations." And further: "Every concretization can be understood as an approximation toward the aim to be attained."[10] Experience shows that in the prevailing majority of cases the human mind recognizes whether the individual decision or the human conduct corresponds to the legal rule (whether the "approximation" is far-going enough for it to be conventionally called as "corresponding" to it).[11] The concept of what today is called a legal

[9] Adolf Merkl, *Die Lehre von der Rechtskraft* (Vienna, 1923), pp. 217 ff.

[10] *Op. cit.*, p. 318. An entirely different view has been expressed by Hermann Isay, *Rechtsnorm und Entscheidung* (Berlin, 1929), p. 5.

[11] Timasheff (*op. cit.*, p. 318) writes that "The detailed study of these functional relations belongs to the most interesting special tasks of the sociology of law to be monographically studied." It should be added that such a study is the prerequisite of a "really realistic" general jurisprudence.

system implies the ability of the individual, whose conduct is directly or indirectly determined by the rule, to ascertain whether or not the rule, which presents itself as a legal one, is (by being covered directly or indirectly by the constitution) a *legal* rule. This assumption presumes the provision for a legal process and a specific machine which makes such an ascertaining at least potentially possible. It presumes a given legal, economic, and political position which makes it possible for the individual to test the rules which allege to be legal. In other words, it presumes implementation and regulation in this regard. From this point of view the concept of a legal system does not admit of an absolute individual obedience, nor the conferring of unspecified powers upon an agency. It has to recognize the individual's inquiry into the nature of supposed-to-be legal rules. That is why a rule system where the sole test of the existence of the rule is given by its physical enforceability, or by its having been enforced by an organized power, is not regarded as a legal system. In the legal sense this recognition of the individual as a legal entity corresponds to the concept of "inalienable human rights" in the political sense. To be sure, this recognition does not imply that the sole subject matter of the legal order is the securing of the economic and political position of the individual. It does not change the principle that the subject matter of the legal order is *social* conduct in the sense of social co-operation of persons as legally recognized entities. A rule system based exclusively on force and fear cannot afford to recognize the individual's being entitled to ascertain the legality of a rule. However, even a very well-developed legal system of a so-called legal state cannot give a perfectly satisfactory solution to this problem. There are only degrees of perfection in a legal system.

To answer the crucial question "Quis custodiet custodes ipsos" according to the requirements of a perfectly secure legal order may lead (to the unconcealed pleasure of apologists of despotic political doctrines) to a vicious spiral of legal reasoning. Admitting that we have not been able to set up a perfect legal order does not in itself contradict the assumption that a rule system which generally prevents the individual from finding out the sequence of facts which verify the legality of a rule or of a fact is not called a legal system.[12] Practical reasons require reasonable limitations in the working of the system of verification, i.e., identifying a rule as a legal rule. There may be agencies set up with a very broad jurisdiction whose acts—according to the legal order itself—are subject to verification only

[12] That is why I agree with Bodenheimer's assumption (*op. cit.*, p. 291): "In order to ascertain whether a certain social order is an order of law, the actual distribution of rights, duties, and powers within the private as well as within the public sphere must be examined."

in very narrow limits. There may be times of emergency when the legal system itself restricts the functioning of the supervisory machine. And even in normal times the smooth operation of the legal system may require compliance with rules which only subsequently can be tested as to their legality. Such rules may be regarded as legal rules with a conditional or limited finality. In other words, the legal system may vest in rules a preliminary legality (existence) for the immediate occasion of maintaining the operation of the legal machine,[13] pending the possibility and result of later supervision. Especially in the service and functioning of military, naval, and police forces such prima-facie validity of commands is necessary. Dicey discussed with dramatic force the legal and personal position of a soldier who may "be liable to be shot by a court martial if he disobeys an order, and to be hanged by a judge and jury if he obeys it."[14] The legal recognition of self-help and self-defense, pending the possibility of later testing the legality of the acts performed under this particular title, may be discussed from this aspect also. The main reason for these apparent deficiencies is due to the necessity of time for the investigation of whether or not a rule or a fact is a legal one.[15] Thus the element of a legal system discussed

[13] Mr. Justice Cardozo quoted such cases.—*The Nature of the Judicial Process*, p. 147. Cf. Holland, *op. cit.*, p. 65.

[14] *Law of the Constitution* (London, 1926), p. 299.

[15] Such a procedure may take many years. The questioning of

here—although essential for its concept—exists only in degrees, like some other elements which we are going to discuss later on.

The proposition that legal acts must be recognizably linked to the legal system implies that the performers of legal acts have to be authorized by legal rules. Such authorization must not be unlimited or so hazy as to be unrecognizable as to the substance of the jurisdiction.[16] Let us look at one example.

G. Jèze, the famous French jurist, expounded a doctrine concerning the acts of usurpers and explained how their acts may become legal acts. He justified his doctrine on the basis of the danger to the social order, "le degré du peril social," which could arise if the acts of an usurper who publicly exercises his function for a long time were not recognized as legal acts. The decisive point with Jèze is the "raison de l'utilité publique."[17] The doctrine of Jèze is inconsistent in that it tries to inject into the legal system extra-legal elements in an extraor-

whether the pre-existing factual situation should be measured according to the legal situation corresponding in time to the factual situation leads to many involved problems.

[16] Roscoe Pound writes about "social control by the judicial process operating according to the law."—*Contemporary Juristic Theory*, p. 53. Morris R. Cohen (*Law and the Social Order*, p. 207) puts the question: "And do not courts themselves operate under law?" Mr. Justice Holmes mentioned in another connection "the rules by which one (the court) is bound."—*Collected Legal Papers*, p. 292.

[17] *Les Principes généraux du droit administratif, La Notion de service public* (Paris, 1930), pp. 285-400. Cf. Ernst Freund, *op. cit.*, pp. 353, 390; James Hart, *An Introduction to Administrative Law* (New York, 1940), pp. 39 ff.

dinary way. Jèze's doctrine falls under the heading of the so-called theory of invalid acts, which has been much discussed in continental Europe.[18] The continental doctrine of administrative law distinguishes between the absolute nullity of a legal act (a non-act) and an invalid act which is presumed to be existent (valid) until it is declared void (ex tunc or ex nunc) by the appropriate authority.[19]

A legal rule necessarily expresses the legal consequences of certain acts and situations happening to occur in the external world.[20] They may relate either to situations which existed before the legal rule was created (ex post facto laws) or to possible future situations. Even though a legal rule expresses the legal consequences of facts and situations which were in existence at or before the creation of the rule, it may express these past acts and situations hypothetically. "Legal rules contain always hypothetical judgments even if they do not appear in such a form," taught Professor Rickert.[21] Some legal

[18] Japiot, *Les Nullités en matière d'acte juridique* (Paris, 1909), *passim;* Walter Jellinek, *Verwaltungsrecht*, p. 262.

[19] See H. Walker, *op. cit.*, p. 420.

[20] They are "the threats," as Dr. Roscoe Pound calls them.—*Contemporary Juristic Theory*, p. 38. W. A. Robson (*op. cit.*, p. 335) cites the following sentences of Thomas Huxley: "But the juridical law is not the cause which makes a man pay his taxes or abstain from one of these crimes. The law is no more than a statement of what will happen to a man who does not pay his taxes or who commits theft or murder."

[21] *Zur Lehre von der Definition* (Tübingen, 1929), p. 33. The same opinion was expressed by Rudolf Stammler, *Theorie der Rechtswissenschaft* (Halle a. d. S., 1923), p. 345.

rules or rule fragments have often been expressed in the form of commands.[22] For instance, Paragraph 138, Title 2 of the *Code of the Laws of the United States* (1934) reads: "The law library shall be open every day so long as either house of congress is in session." From a legal point of view this sentence has to be completed by a statement of the legal consequences of the hypothetically stated situation or fact that the librarian will not comply with the requirements set forth in it. Such a rule may be expressed in still another way: for example, "If the librarian does not hold open the Library of Congress every day so long as either house of congress is in session, a determined authority releases an order to deduct . . . from his bond each time." The second form expresses the legal consequences together with the hypothetically stated factual situation. The logical difference between a hypothetical judgment and a command is not important as long as a *legal* command contains or relates to the legal consequences of noncompliance with the command. In a legal sense *behind* any hypothetical judgment is always a desirable human social conduct. Austin[23] regarded a legal rule as a species of command carrying legal consequences.

[22] A. Kocourek (*op. cit.*, p. 142) writes: "A legal rule is an abstract command to do an act with a threat of sanction." Professor Kocourek (*op. cit.*, p. 144) names two essential elements of a legal rule: (1) hypothesis duties (the duties of the subjects) and (2) disposition powers (of the government).

[23] *Op. cit.*, I, 98 f.

A legal order may define its own legal rule and in this way communicate what is meant in the *particular* legal order by the expression "legal rule" or "law." Such definitions apparently do not change the elements of what is called a legal system or a legal rule. The proverb "Caesar non supra grammaticos"[24] well expresses the limitations of legislation pertaining to this point. However, such definitions greatly influence common usage and thus, within certain limitations, the legal order whose agencies become "supra grammaticos." A legal system may define what the terms used in legal rules mean.[25]

The concept of the legal order implies that, in the prevailing majority of cases, people comply with the rules without their enforcement. I do not explain this fact as dependent upon the "recognition" of the legal rules in the sense of Bierling.[26] Cases in which the legal rules must be enforced because people are not complying with them must remain

[24] Kelsen, *Legal Technique in International Law*, p. 21; Somlo, *op. cit.*, pp. 185 ff.; Morris R. Cohen, *op. cit.*, p. 206.

[25] See W. H. McClenon and W. C. Gilbert, *Index to Federal Statutes, 1874-1931* (Washington, 1933), list of statutory definitions, pp. 1127-35.

[26] Cf. Somlo, *op. cit.*, pp. 138 f., 434 f. Somlo expounded the doctrines of Bierling and John Austin with reference to the recognition of the legal rules as condition of their being called so. Although a positive attitude of the people toward the legal *system* is one of the system's essential features, the statement that each single legal rule has to be recognized by the people seems to be an exaggerated assumption of the requirement that legal rules have to be regularly complied with.

relatively rare.[27] We may suppose that the very fact that a great number of legal rules must be enforced would mean the destruction of the legal system as a whole.[28] Law enforcement presupposes a state monopoly[29] in using physical power in maintaining the legal order. The maintenance of this monopoly requires an institutionalized machine which virtually or actually is powerful enough to defend the political life of the nation according to the legal order, that is, according to the political will of the self-preference[30] of the nation.

The knowableness of the rules pertaining to a legal system is today an element of what is called a legal order, just as the requirement of habitual compliance with the legal rules is. Similarly, as it is not absolutely necessary that *all* legal rules in a legal system without exception be complied with, so the legal rules must only be *generally* knowable.[31]

[27] Timasheff (*op. cit.,* p. 4) writes: ". . . the triumph of the social force called law is the rule, the definite defeat of law merely an exception."

[28] Max A. Shepard ("An Analysis of Analytical Jurisprudence," 1 *Journal of Politics* 381), considering Bentham's definition of law as not realistic, wrote that "law must be regarded as a seamless web of rules and as that complex of social norms generally obeyed."

[29] This monopolistic position is emphasized by Thomas Hobbes, characterizing the "mortal god," by quoting on the title page of his *Leviathan* the biblical words, "Non est potestas super terram quae comparetur ei."

[30] See Mr. Justice Holmes, *The Common Law,* p. 44.

[31] As early as in 1689 the British Bill of Rights brought the charge against the British kings that their behavior was "utterly and directly contrary to the *known* laws and statutes. . . ." See R. K. Gooch, *Source Book on the Government of England,* p. 90.

A legal system may contain relatively few rules which are not generally knowable, but the prevailing majority of legal rules must be knowable[32] in order for a rule system to be called a legal system; and even these relatively few rules must not be cardinal rules which vitally influence main groups of rules in the frame of a legal system. To be sure, a particular legal system may prescribe within its own jurisdiction that particular legal rules be communicated to certain persons and may make the validity (existence) of a legal rule dependent on the fulfillment of this condition. Whereas being manifested is a prerequisite of a heteronomous rule (and the legal rule is always a heteronomous rule), general knowability is not an elementary requirement of *each* legal rule. However, legal orders of highly civilized nations with a democratic form of government provide all possible means for making the legal rules knowable. The defense of the country, foreign relations, monetary policy, and the like may be regarded as reasons for not making legal rules generally knowable, even in democracies. Such not-generally-knowable legal rules are *manifested* by the proper authorities; but they are knowable only to *certain* persons. They may establish consequences for the conduct of persons who were not in a posi-

[32] John Dickinson ("A Working Theory of Sovereignty," 42 *Pol. Sc. Quar.* 525) speaks of a capableness of "being known with some degree of accuracy in advance."

tion to foretell the consequences of their conduct.[33] Kant[34] regarded the publicity of legal rules as a positive requirement both from the ethical and juridical point of view.[35]

The general knowableness of court decisions is of an immense political importance not only as a means of making public sign vehicles of general legal rules but also as a vigorous political instrument in popular participation in governmental control.

A legal order is established for an indefinite time,[36] whereas legal rules may be instituted for a predetermined future time period. Virtually, the legal rule has in the process of time a beginning, a time period of existence, and an end. The beginning of a legal rule must be characterized by the appearance

[33] Jerome Frank (*Law and the Modern Mind* [New York, 1936], p. 35) expressed the opinion that "most men act without regard to the legal consequences of their conduct, and, therefore, do not act in reliance upon any given pre-existing law."

[34] *Perpetual Peace* (American Peace Society ed., Boston, 1897), p. 46. Cf. Kelsen, *Hauptprobleme der Staatsrechtslehre* (Tübingen, 1923), p. 280; E. Schiffer, *Die deutsche Justiz* (Berlin, 1928), pp. 90 f.; Somlo, *op. cit.*, pp. 507 f.

[35] Bentham taught: "Whether a law is written or unwritten it is not less necessary that it should be known." "Caligula," writes Bentham, "suspended the table of his laws upon lofty columns, that he might render the knowledge of them difficult. How numerous are the countries in which matters are still worse."—*View of a Complete Code of Laws*, Chap. xxi, and the former quotation from *Constitutional Code*, Book II, Chap. vii, Sec. V, from *The Works of Jeremy Bentham* (Edinburgh, John Bowring, 1843), III, 205; IX, 201. "Law as a guide of conduct is reduced to the level of mere futility if it is unknown and unknowable."—Cardozo, *The Growth of the Law*, p. 3.

[36] Bentham (*A Fragment on Government*, Chaps. i, xiii, note c, *Works*, I, 264) taught that an indefinite duration of time is essential for a *political* society.

of a sign manifesting the legal rule. The birth of a legal rule cannot always be definitely assigned in the process of time. These rules are made legitimate by their *recognition* as legal rules. The end of the existence of a legal rule must be ascertainable like its beginning. The proposition "lex posterior derogat priori" essentially belongs to each legal system, provided that the lex posterior is qualified according to the constitution to replace the former legal rule. Of course, there are prenatal and posthumous facts related to the legal rule also, but they may become important only with reference to the existence or significance of the legal rule.

In discussing elements of the concept of a legal order, I designated some of them as having to be performed only regularly, admitting exceptions to a certain degree. Such assumptions may be blamed as inconsistent, or as not meeting the insatiable human craving for perfect social institutions. However, my intention has been to describe ever so fragmentarily some points and some processes in which they ought to occur if they are—according to convention —at least in one part of the civilized world, to be called a *legal* system. It seemed vain to me to infer pessimistic deductions owing to our inability to create more perfect social institutions.

V

COURT SYSTEMS AS DETERMINED BY
SPECIFIC LEGAL ORDERS

IT IS A PLATITUDE that the separation of powers[1] has been recommended as a means of protecting political liberty.[2] The tendency of dictatorial regimes to concentrate powers shows that the remedy was well-founded.[3] The intention of the doctrine of the separation of powers was to recommend a particular structure for a "moderate" government: legislative agencies with a legislative function separated from

[1] John Locke (*Of Civil Government*, Book II, Chap. xiii), distinguished the supreme power of the people from the legislative power. The executive and federative "powers" were designated as subordinated to the legislative power. The expression "power" is commonly used to designate "function" or "jurisdiction." Ralph F. Fuchs ("An Approach to Administrative Law," 18 *N. C. Law Rev.* 186 f.) examines the different meanings of the words "power" and "function."

[2] Cf. Montesquieu, *The Spirit of Laws,* Book XI, Chaps. iv, vi; Felix Frankfurter and James M. Landis, "Power of Congress over Procedure in Criminal Contempts in 'Inferior' Federal Courts—A Study in Separation of Powers," 37 *Harv. Law Rev.* 1012 f. Joseph-Barthélemy, *Précis de droit constitutionnel* (Paris, 1938), p. 84. Barthélemy's *Traité de droit constitutionnel* (Paris, 1933), published in collaboration with Paul Duez, is more elaborate; however, his *Précis* is of more recent origin. I quote his *Précis* as often as *Droit constitutionnel.*

[3] As early as 1934 Walter Jellinek, in the supplement to his *Verwaltungsrecht* (p. 4), wrote, in adapting his book to the requirements of the new regime: "The doctrine of separation of powers as an ideal has obviously no room in the antiliberalistic, national-socialist, leader-state." Aristotle (*Politics,* IV, 14, 1298 a) called attention to "well ordered" constitutions in this respect.

executive agencies with an executive function.[4] The executive agencies were divided into two groups: first, agencies with adjudicative functions, called courts,[5] and second, the agencies applying and enforcing legal rules created by the legislature in so far as they are not applied or enforced by the courts.[6] Nonjudicial power was called executive power, although it was known that there was no *logical* difference between the two "executive" functions.[7] To be sure, the framers of doctrines of the separation of powers supposed that there was a clear-cut difference between a general legal rule and a specific decision and that the problem of the division of functions and the allotment of them to particular agencies (the determination of the jurisdiction) was a mere problem of political will and legal technique. The doctrine of the separation of powers decidedly influenced most of the constitutions of the last two centuries. Some of the constitutions expressly contain the political principle of the separation of powers.[8]

[4] The Chinese constitution separates five powers. See Joseph-Barthélemy, *Droit constitutionnel*, p. 83. With reference to the proposal of establishing four departments in all American constitutions, see Roscoe Pound, *Contemporary Juristic Theory*, pp. 12, 13.

[5] "By the third, he punishes criminals, or determines the disputes that arise between individuals."—Montesquieu, *op. cit.*, Book XI, Chap. vi.

[6] "By the second he makes peace or war, sends or receives embassies, establishes the public security, and provides against invasions." —*Ibid.*

[7] Joseph-Barthélemy, *Droit constitutionnel*, p. 83.

[8] For example, Sec. 8 of the constitution of North Carolina reads

Common usage even now applies the terms "legislative," "judicial," and "executive" to designate legal functions (jurisdictions) *and* agencies. Often the functions of agencies have not been categorized according to their substrata, but according to the *name* of the agencies which have the jurisdiction over the matter, and it thus has happened that the function of an agency called a legislative agency has been called a legislative function, the function of an agency called an executive agency, an executive function, and the function of an agency called a judicial agency, a judicial function. Today political and legal doctrine recognizes that the agencies called legislative agencies may have legislative, executive, and judicial functions, and that all three of these functions may be conferred upon judicial and executive agencies too.[9] The terminology as used in various legal systems seems to be rather inconsistent. Legal orders use the expression "legislative function" as a synonym for the creation of rules of general applicability, but sometimes for specific kinds of individual

as follows: "The legislative, executive, and judicial powers distinct: The legislative, executive and supreme judicial powers of the government ought to be forever separate and distinct from each other."

[9] Montesquieu admitted exceptions to the principle of separation of powers in the case of "danger by some secret conspiracy against the state, or by a correspondence with a foreign enemy . . .," thus indicating the modern concept of the delegation of legislative powers in case of emergency.—*Op. cit.*, Book XI, Chap. vi. Concerning the exceptional character of certain powers which, according to the plan of separation of powers, do not belong to the functions of an agency, see O'Donoghue *vs.* U. S., 289 U. S. 516.

legal rules also. The confusion has increased in many countries where, due to extraordinary circumstances, the jurisdiction of the so-called legislative bodies had been conferred upon the executive. Also the executive power has been regarded as separated from the judicial power despite the fact that the finality of the general rules and specific decisions created by executive agencies has been limited by the jurisdiction of courts to review of these rules.[10] Such new expressions as "policy-determining function," "sublegislative function," "quasi-judicial function,"[11] have been introduced to maintain the presumption that legislative agencies perform mostly legislative acts, courts mostly judicial acts, and the other public agencies mostly executive (and administrative) acts.[12] The development of a doctrine concerning governmental acts which have not been regarded as being subject to court supervision, and the recognition of non-authoritative administrative acts, through which a

[10] See Kenneth C. Cole, " 'Government,' 'Law' and the Separation of Powers," 33 *Amer. Pol. Sc. Rev.* 424.

[11] The meaning of the expression "quasi-judicial" as used in the British legal doctrine is discussed in the *Report of the Committee on Ministers' Powers* (London, H. M. Stationery Office, 1936), pp. 93 f., hereafter referred to as *Sankey Report*.

[12] The provisions enacted by the American Congress for the reorganization of the executive departments of the United States declare (Sec. 401 of Title 4, part 2) to be the policy of Congress: "(d) to segregate regulatory agencies and functions from those of an administrative and executive character." James W. Fesler introduces his paper, "Independence of State Regulatory Agencies" (34 *Amer. Pol. Sc. Rev.* 935), with the sentence: "Transference to administrative agencies of powers traditionally associated with legislatures and with courts has destroyed old categories of political science. . . ."

public agency does not present itself as an "authority" in the proper sense, occasioned a new cleavage and a new "separation" within the executive power.[18] The methods of public administration by "nonauthoritative" acts (as the purchasing of commodities by contracts, etc.) and by the establishment of public and private agencies and corporations which provide social control by promotion of education, construction and maintaining of highways, the management of public property, and so on, seemed to complicate the classical concept of the executive power by introducing the notion of noncoercive forms of administrative actions. Walter Jellinek distinguished between authoritative forms of public administration (Obrigkeitliche Verwaltung) and noncoercive public administration (Schlichte Hoheitsverwaltung or nicht-obrigkeitliche Verwaltung).[14] The French doctrine made a similar distinction. In the last decades the "actes de gestion," which do not cover exactly the German concept of nonauthoritative public administrative acts, have been subjected to the super-

[18] See Louis Roland, *Précis de droit administratif* (Paris, 1938), pp. 60-63. With reference to the American doctrine of the judicial review of "political questions," see State of Georgia *vs.* Stanton, 6 Wall 50 (1867). See also Lauterpacht, *op. cit.,* pp. 387 ff., and Charles Gordon Post, *The Supreme Court and Political Questions* ("The Johns Hopkins University Studies in Historical and Political Science," Series LIV, No. 4. Baltimore, 1936). Dr. Post discusses (pp. 98-99) the view of Field (8 *Minn. Law Rev.* 511) that the courts cannot decide "political" questions because "where no rules exist the court is powerless to act."

[14] *Op. cit.,* pp. 20-22.

vision of administrative courts by the changed attitude of the Council of State.

A complication with reference to the conception of the executive power arose in attempting to distinguish between the "rule of law" and the so-called "administrative law" on the one side, and between law and public administration as two categories of state functions on the other. The first distinction related to the difference between the classical French-German-Italian system of public administration (including the system of review of administrative acts by specific courts) and between the British-American system of public administration, including the principle of review of all administrative acts by ordinary courts. The second distinction relates to the kinds of discretionary power conferred upon administrative agencies and courts and to the working methods of the two sets of agencies.

The system of the highly centralized Napoleonic form of public administration and the nonsupervision of acts of the executive power by any courts, or their review by specific administrative courts, has been called by Dicey the system of "droit administratif." In the preface to his first edition of the *Introduction to the Study of the Law of the Constitution* we find the characteristic accusation "that the views of the prerogative maintained by Crown lawyers under the Tudors and the Stuarts bear a marked resemblance to the legal and administrative ideas which at the present day under the Third Republic still support the droit administratif of France."[15] Although Dicey considerably modified his opinion,[16] recognizing that "the droit administratif of France is year by year becoming more and more judicialized,"[17] the Lord Chief Justice, Lord Hewart of Bury, in 1929 in his famous book *The New Despotism* pointed out that "Between the 'Rule of Law' and what is called 'administrative law' (happily there is no English name for it) there is the sharpest possible contrast. One is substantially the opposite of the other."[18]

Dicey well recognized the consequences of the impact of the Napoleonic system upon the problem of the obedience of public administrative agencies and public officials to executive orders. He compared it rightly with the situation of English soldiers.[19] Indeed, neither the Continental admin-

[15] (London, 1926), p. vii, first edition published in 1885.

[16] Cf. Felix Frankfurter, "The Task of Administrative Law," *Law and Politics* (New York, 1939), p. 232, originally published in 75 *Penna. Law Rev.* 614 (1927). However, the view of Dicey regarding the French system as inexpedient for the British legal order remained unchanged. According to the *Sankey Report* (p. 111), presented to Parliament in 1932, "Professor Dicey's conclusion is no less true today than it was in 1915." Quoting the article of Dicey, "The Development of Administrative Law in England" (31 *Law Quart. Rev.* 148), the Sankey Committee concurred in the opinion that the rule of law "was fatal to the existence of true droit administratif." See W. A. Robson, *Justice and Administrative Law* (London, 1928), *passim;* James M. Landis, *The Administrative Process* (New Haven, 1938), *passim.*

[17] *Op. cit.,* p. xliv.

[18] (London, 1929), p. 37. Lord Hewart's opinion was adopted by the Committee on Ministers' Powers (*Sankey Report,* p. 110).

[19] *Op. cit.,* p. 354. Cf. Hewart, *op. cit.,* p. 39.

istrative-law doctrine nor positive legal regulations have yet succeeded in formulating a workable conception of the duty of executive officials to verify the legality of an order given by their superiors.[20] The French droit administratif succeeded in evolving a satisfactory doctrine and practice concerning the protection of individuals against arbitrary administrative action, including compensation for injuries caused by unlawful *or* arbitrary action. The concept of arbitrariness as defined by the Council of State has to be regarded as very effective with reference to the legal protection of the individual.

To be sure, Lord Hewart considers droit administratif as "a definite system of law, the rules and principles of which . . . differ essentially from the rules and principles of the ordinary law governing the relations of private citizens inter se."[21] Administrative law (which I regard as the English translation for droit administratif) is, in my opinion, a branch of the legal system as are civil law and crim-

[20] Paul Laband (*Das Staatsrecht des Deutschen Reiches* [Tübingen, 1911], I, 461) taught that every public officer has necessarily to verify at his own risk whether or not an order of his superior corresponds to the law. The former Austrian Constitution as amended in 1925 prescribed that an officer is bound by the order of his superior unless it conflicts with criminal laws or unless the authority who gave the order had no jurisdiction over the subject matter to which the order relates. Otto Mayer (*Deutsches Verwaltungsrecht* [München, 1924], II, 182 ff.) adopted generally the view of Laband but admitted only very narrow practical limits to the examination of the legality of administrative orders. Professor Mayer emphasized that Otto Laband regarded the relationship between authority and officer as based also on force (Gewaltverhältnis).

[21] *Op. cit.*, pp. 41-42.

inal law; although "this illegitimate exotic, administrative law, almost overnight overwhelmed the profession . . . ," to cite the words of Mr. Justice Frankfurter.[22] The expression "administrative rule" has been defined in an interesting manner by the "Bill, To provide for the more expeditious settlement of disputes with the United States and for other purposes." The definition, given only "for the purposes of that particular act," reads: "'Administrative rules' include rules, regulations, orders, and amendments thereto of general application issued by officers in the executive branch of the United States government interpreting the terms of statutes they are respectively charged with administering."[23]

Edgar Bodenheimer, in a recent study referring to Dr. Roscoe Pound, designates law and administration as two "rival agencies." "Law and administration are different not only in their concept, but also in their operation and effect," according to him. "Law is mainly concerned with rights, administration is mainly concerned with results."[24] Dr. Bodenheimer—discussing the pertinent opinions of George Jellinek, Paul Laband, E. Paschukanis, and the opposing view of H. Kelsen—assumes that public administration "is a sphere of free activity by the

[22] "The Task of Administrative Law," *Law and Politics,* p. 233.
[23] H. R. 6198, 75th Cong., 1st Sess.
[24] *Jurisprudence* (New York, 1940), p. 95. Cf. Homer Cummings, *Liberty under Law and Administration* (New York, 1934), pp. 130 f.; John Dickinson, "Government versus Law," *Administrative Justice,* Chap. I.

government with the guiding principle of expediency and of achieving practical results."[25]   However, public administration is "limited" by law, according to Bodenheimer.[26]   I doubt whether the distinction between law and administration is very clear or fortunate with reference to *general* jurisprudence.[27]   I suppose that the means by which human social conduct is influenced directly and indirectly through legal rules are many and various.   I even admit that a new method of the division of legal functions would be very desirable, but I do not believe that *besides* law "There is *another* instrument of social regulation, which is called administration," as Bodenheimer put it.[28]   John D. O'Reilly is right when he states that "administration without, or contrary

[25] *Jurisprudence*, p. 91.   [26] *Ibid.*

[27] Dr. Roscoe Pound teaches "that something more than history was involved in our inherited attitude toward administration," referring to Anglo-American legal history.—"Individualization of Justice," 7 *Fordh. Law Rev.* 159. Page 160 of the same study contains a significant distinction between judicial and administrative discretion. With reference to the distinction of administrative and judicial powers in Athens, see R. J. Bonner and G. Smith, *The Administration of Justice from Homer to Aristotle* (Chicago, 1938), II, 304.

[28] *Op. cit.*, p. 86. (My italics.) It is true that at present legal systems operate with several kinds of "instruments." One group of instruments operates according to the administrative process; another group, according to the judicial process. Both are *equally* determined by "law." There is a hierarchical relationship between law and public administration; they are not co-ordinated instruments. That is why I am opposing the formulation of Dr. Bodenheimer: "Morals, customs and law are not the only agencies of social control in modern society. There is . . . another instrument of social regulation, which is called administration." I do not think that the pertinent doctrines of G. Jellinek and Laband, as quoted by Bodenheimer, fit in the modern conception of a legal system.

to, 'law' may be, and probably is, an entirely different thing from administration without, or contrary to, the 'general' or 'common' law."[29] However, such reasoning does not take into account the fact that common law cannot exist in conflict with other legal rules. I agree with Professor O'Reilly that "administration without law" and "administration contrary to law," as used in the sixth report of the Special Committee on Administrative Law of the American Bar Association, should be interpreted in this way.

The above mentioned discussion may be simplified by avoiding the use of the term "law" as designating judicial power or the judicial process in contrast to public administration or the administrative process. This seems to be necessary, on the one hand, to eliminate the impression that law does not embrace public administration or the administrative process, on the other hand, to remove the possible misunderstandings involved in the employment of such ambiguous terms as "law." I assume that it suffices to say—as Roscoe Pound so clearly expressed it—that law is the exercising of social control "through a judicial and an administrative process carried on in accordance with a body of authoritative precepts and an authoritative technique."[30] This is not to say that

[29] "Administrative Absolutism," 7 *Fordh. Law Rev.* 313.

[30] *Contemporary Juristic Theory*, pp. 16-17. H. Lauterpacht (*op. cit.*, p. 386) writes: ". . . The view that administrative justice constitutes a limitation upon the rule of law cannot be admitted as a sound legal proposition. . . . Administrative agencies, so long as they do not act illegally, administer the law. . . . It is a mistake to assume

there are no differences between the two processes
and techniques. They have been discussed by Professor Pound many times.[31] He and many other
authors emphasized in regard to both processes that
the diagnosis whether or not coercive realities are
law or lawful cannot be found by the mere determination whether an act is performed by men called
public officials, but by the nature of its relationship
to a legal rule system. It should be added—as mentioned many times in this paper—that general legal
rules may be complied with without any judicial or
administrative process in an active sense.[32] In such
cases these processes represent potential energy which
may be converted into positive action.

It is a platitude to state that the dogma of the
separation of powers is conceived differently in each
particular legal order. Joseph-Barthélemy assumes
that "the idea of Montesquieu in the American political language has taken on a mechanical aspect, that
is by the system of checks and balances."[33] It should
be emphasized that this so-called "mechanical" aspect

that ordinary courts administer rules of law, whereas administrative
agencies act according to discretion."

[31] For example, "Individualization of Justice," 7 *Fordh. Law Rev.*
160 ff.

[32] Whereas I regard as the main function of legal rules the influencing of the social behavior of the "law-abiding citizen" in his
everyday life (beside other auxiliary functions), Gerhard Husserl opines
that "Cases which call for a legal handling are in the *first* place what
we may call *pathological* situations, i.e., social events which radically
disrupt convention, such as murder, arson, robbery, etc."—"Everyday
Life and the Law," 5 *Social Philosophy* 309-25. (My italics.)

[33] *Droit constitutionnel*, p. 84.

in political language may be found in David Hume too, who, in his famous essay, "That Politics May be Reduced to a Science," spoke of "particular checks and controls" which a republican and a free government should provide.[34] Without attempting to analyze the political and legal conceptions of the doctrine of separation of powers, and especially not its American conception,[35] it seems to be necessary to make clear the fact that the American doctrine differs in some main points from the many European conceptions of it.[36]

The separation of the judicial power from the other two traditional governmental functions naturally requires an adequately accurate concept of what is called judicial power. The proverb "Qui bene

[34] *Essays Moral, Political and Literary* (London, 1898), I, 99. Cf. Woodrow Wilson, *Constitutional Government in the United States* (New York, 1908), pp. 199, 203-4, 221-22.

[35] Roscoe Pound assumes that the lines of the American constitutional separation of powers "seem now reasonably well established."— 7 *Fordh. Law Rev.* 161.

[36] The Earl of Balfour, introducing the new edition of Walter Bagehot's *The English Constitution* (London, Oxford Press, 1933, p. xi), writes that the British Constitution "certainly does not suffer from too elaborate a system of checks and balances." According to Balfour, "When unity and rapidity of national action were required, the country would have to trust to the political genius of its people rather than to the formal machinery provided for it by the constitution." The differences in doctrine have been accentuated by Robert Jennings Harris, *The Judicial Power of the United States* (Baton Rouge, 1940), p. 1. Professor Harris distinguished between the United States and "other states possessing a representative form of government where the dogma of the separation of powers must yield to the doctrine of legislative supremacy. Parliamentary sovereignty implies judicial subjection in the sense that it tends to render courts an instrument of the administrative machinery. . . ."

distinguit, bene docet" particularly relates to this matter. Conceiving the judicial machine and the judicial process as pertaining to the legal system, contrasted with a superlegal conception, we have necessarily to infer that the judicial power is determined by the *particular* legal system of a country.[37] The legal rules determining the judicial power are interpreted according to the common (political and legal) usage of a country,[38] which is decidedly influenced by the interpretation of the constitution by the highest courts. It is a well-known fact that the judicial power is regulated rather differently in each particular state (even among democracies), and that the political position of the judiciary has been greatly influenced by the political traditions of each nation. Take, for instance, the views on the legal position of American, French, and British courts. American courts are very highly esteemed;[39] they are recog-

[37] With reference to the United States, R. J. Harris (*op. cit.,* pp. 1-2) writes: "The courts have achieved a degree of independence from statutory regulation and control that exists in no other country." Concerning the organization and history of American courts, see Roscoe Pound, *Organization of Courts* (Boston, 1940), *passim.*

[38] R. J. Harris (*op. cit.,* pp. 2 f.) illustrates with many examples his assumption that "By judicial decision the term 'judicial power' has been gradually converted into a symbol which partakes of mystical and transcendental attributes emanating from the doctrine of the separation of powers and its corollary, the independence of the judiciary."

[39] "Americans venerate their judiciary. And that is as it should be."—Frank T. Hogan, President of the American Bar Association, 25 *Amer. Bar. Assoc. Journ.* 629. A. S. Beardsley (*op. cit.,* p. 94) writes with reference to American courts, "Decisions of courts are the words of final authority as to what is or is not the law. Thus, in the adjudication of controverted questions, judicial decisions do two things:

nized as guardians over the constitution and review acts of the executive power as to their legality. In France the ordinary courts have been regarded as ordinary public agencies without any jurisdiction to review acts of the legislative power. The three fundamental laws of 1875, which have been called the written constitution of France, did not even mention courts or the judicial power. No wonder that one of the most respected scholars of French constitutional law, Joseph-Barthélemy, teaches that one of the *main* principles of the French public law is the distrust of the judiciary: "la méfiance du judiciaire."[40] In Great Britain the judiciary is held in high esteem, and has a firmly rooted universally-known tradition.[41] However, the court system is slightly com-

(1) they declare the law on points not covered by legislation, or (2) they determine, by judicial construction, the ultimate effect of the provisions of constitutions and statutes. This exposition and interpretation of the law *becomes binding* upon *every citizen* within the court's jurisdiction, while *the law of the decision becomes a part of the public law of the state.*" (My italics.)

[40] *Précis de droit constitutionnel*, p. 121. The reasons for the traditional distrust of the French judiciary have been discussed by Henry Leyret in the introduction to his *Les Jugements du Président Magnaud* (Paris, 1900). Leyret characterizes President Magnaud ("le bon juge!") as a judge who replaced the written law by the law of nature, the dogma by reason, and the code by justice.—P. xxiv. The development of the popular concept of "le bon juge," the idea of a judge who decides cases according to justice and not only according to the law, is very significant in this connection.

[41] How far this doctrine goes may be seen by reading H. J. Laski's answer to the question: "How far, firstly, can the courts allow their jurisdiction to be ousted on the ground of military necessity?"—*A Grammar of Politics* (New Haven, 1931), pp. 554-55. The significance of the role of the courts in the evolution of the British Constitution is emphasized by W. S. Holdsworth, introducing his *History of*

plicated by the judicial functions of the House of Lords and of the Privy Council. There is no guardianship over acts of Parliament. The jurisdiction of British courts as to the review of acts of the executive power is very extensive but not general. The way in which the report of the British Committee on Ministers' Powers (Sankey Report) discusses certain decisions of the executive power is peculiarly significant. It calls certain decisions of administrative agencies "truly judicial," though not given by a "Court of Law," and expresses the opinion that "sheltering them from the 'Courts of Law' by an immunity of supervision is contrary to the British Constitution."[42] However, I assume that the expression "contrary to the the British Constitution" should be interpreted as: contrary to British political tradition.

Felix Frankfurter and James M. Landis examined the problems arising from the vagueness of the term "judicial power."[43] They wrote, with reference to the American Constitution, that "the Constitution has prescribed very little in determining the content, and guiding the exercise of judicial power."[44] Dis-

English Law (Boston, 1922, I, 1) by the sentence: "Legal history therefore must always begin with the history of courts."

[42] *Sankey Report,* pp. 74, 108. Cf. the rather significant opinion contained in the decision of British Imperial Oil Co., Ltd., *vs.* Federal Commissioner of Taxation, quoted by Felix Frankfurter and Harry Shulman, *Cases and Other Authorities on Federal Jurisdiction and Procedure* (Chicago, 1937), pp. 117 ff.

[43] "Power of Congress," 37 *Harv. Law Rev.* 1010.

[44] *Ibid.,* p. 1018.

cussing the jurisdiction of inferior federal courts, of removing obstacles which hinder the effectiveness of their work, Frankfurter and Landis scrutinized the meaning of the expression "inherent power" as related to courts.[45] Both authors emphasized how often problems of the division of political powers are in the background of apparently simple jurisdictional issues.[46]

In this paper, which is concerned with a few characteristic points of the American doctrine of the judicial power in so far as they are particularly significant from the point of view of general jurisprudence, I naturally do not attempt to describe or to criticize even briefly the American doctrine itself. However, the reader will notice that typical American problems mirror and often elucidate general legal problems in a very significant manner.[47] How the legal position and jurisdictional problems of courts influence "the most vital intellectual problems of the law" is stressed by Felix Frankfurter and Wilbur G. Katz in the Introduction to the original edition of their *Cases and Other Authorities on Federal Jurisdiction and Procedure.*[48]

[45] *Ibid.*, p. 1023. R. J. Harris (*op. cit.*, p. 145) writes: "Such powers exist because of the belief that they inhere in judicial tribunals as an incident of their creation and existence as courts."

[46] *The Business of the Supreme Court* (New York, 1928), p. 2.

[47] See, for example, the distinctions made by Thurman W. Arnold in *The Symbols of Government* (New Haven, 1935, pp. 205-6) between courts, commissions, and bureaus.

[48] (Chicago, 1931), p. v.

Perhaps one of the most decisive points concerning the place of courts in a legal system is shown by their position with respect to the legislative power, that is, whether or not the courts are in charge of reviewing all acts of the so-called "legislative power" as to their constitutionality.

According to Professor Kocourek, the power of the courts of the United States not to apply unconstitutional statutes "lies in the unwritten supremacy of the judiciary."[49] I understand this assumption to mean that the unwritten part of the American Constitution entitles only the judiciary to examine authoritatively whether statutes were created by the legislative agencies according to the Constitution, whereas statutory rules have to be complied with by ordinary people and other agencies until they are (perhaps) found to be unconstitutional by a court. One may explain the duty of courts to apply *only* (in accordance with the Constitution) to existent laws by assuming that the applying of a legal rule implies the duty of examining whether there is an existing rule. Although this assumption seems to be consistent with a legal "order," it is complicated, on the one hand, by the question whether only courts are charged with the verification of the existence of statutory law, in contrast to other public agencies and ordinary people; on the other hand, by the fact that the legal systems of many democracies

[49] *Op. cit.,* p. 107. See O. P. Field, *The Effect of an Unconstitutional Statute* (Minneapolis, 1935), *passim.*

do not permit anybody to examine the constitutionality of acts of legislative bodies. On first thought
one assumes that the decision of the court, declaring
an act of the legislative bodies existent or nonexistent, relates only to the particular case which was
decided. However, the problem is whether the non-
recognition of the constitutionality of the statute by
the court applies *generally* to people; that is, whether
other people are prevented from complying with the
statute which in a *particular* case was declared unconstitutional. In other words, whether the compliance with such a "statute" is unlawful for people
to whom the individual decision does not apply.

Joseph-Barthélemy quotes Lambert's statement
that the American system creates an uncertainty as to
whether statutes exist at all. Mr. Barthélemy, referring to the *Kansas City Star* (May 11, 1930), points
out that Americans consider their Supreme Court a
branch of the legislative power.[50] I believe that
Joseph-Barthélemy is wrong in assuming that the so-
called uncertainty is created "by the American legal
system." As to uncertainty, one should realize that
as long as a state exists there is either a higher or a
lesser *degree* of legal certainty (or a higher or lesser
degree of uncertainty). Political experience shows

[50] *Précis de droit constitutionnel,* pp. 119-20. The quoted book of
E. Lambert is *Le Gouvernement des juges et la lutte contre la législa-
tion sociale aux États-Unis* (Paris, 1922). E. A. Radice (*Fundamental
Issues in the United States* [Oxford, 1936], p. 33) points out that
Americans "have sometimes regarded the Supreme Court as a third
chamber with the power of vetoing certain acts of Congress."

that the American system affords not *absolute cer-tainty* but a high *degree* of constitutional certainty. Other constitutions also regulate or prohibit the authoritative examination of the constitutionality of acts of legislative bodies. The few European states which, preceding the present political upheaval, adopted the system of court guardianship over the constitution, applied several devices for ascertaining the constitutionality of acts of legislative bodies. One of them is the system whereby *specific* courts examine the question of constitutionality. Joseph-Barthélemy cites some well-known examples.[51] He also names countries which have adopted the American system,[52] discussing both systems with a certain skepticism and defending the French system of the supremacy of the legislative body.[53] In Weimar Germany, the problem of the guardianship of the courts over the acts of legislative bodies was discussed hotly in 1924. The members of one of the chambers of the German Supreme Court in Leipzig initiated a petition of the Association of German Judges to the German Government, addressed to the Minister of Justice, calling attention to the fact that there was a danger that the German courts would, by reason of conflict with the rule of morals and as a consequence of this conflict, declare as void a statute which was at this time planned by the Ger-

[51] *Droit constitutionnel*, pp. 117-18.   [52] *Ibid.*, p. 120.
[53] *Précis de droit public* (Paris, 1937), pp. 270, 291-95.

man Government. The proposed statute contained regulations pertaining to the rapid depreciation of the German currency. In reply to this petition the German Minister of Justice declared emphatically that it would lead to a *dissolution* of the German legal order if German courts supposed themselves to be entitled not to apply a statute created in accordance with the constitution, giving as reason that the majority of the members of the court were of the opinion that the statute conflicted with rules of morals, and was therefore void. Seemingly, the members of the Reichsgericht adopted the view of the Minister of Justice.[54] E. A. Radice is probably right in assuming that "the permanent achievement of the United States lies in the fact that she has evolved a working legal mechanism to settle conflicts which in Europe may lead to the use of force, or, at any rate, to constant friction or ill feeling."[55]

An agency can be established *only* by legal rules determining its jurisdiction.[56] This jurisdiction may be narrow or broad, but it must be determined by

[54] See T. Jastrow, *Die Prinzipienfragen in den Aufwertungsdebatten* (Brünn, 1937), p. 11.

[55] *Op. cit.*, p. 5.

[56] I am using the term jurisdiction to designate the *legal* functions of a public agency as determined by legal rules. Professor Kocourek distinguishes between "competence" and "jurisdiction," stating that "Jurisdiction is made up both of lawful and unlawful powers."—*An Introduction to the Science of Law*, p. 325. It cannot be denied that "The direction may be implied, however, as well as expressed."— Benjamin N. Cardozo, *The Paradoxes of Legal Science*, p. 28, analyzing the doctrine of Stammler. The relationship between courts and the law is discussed by Cardozo in *The Growth of the Law*, p. 49.

formulated, manifested sentences, and it must not be subject to original determination by the agencies themselves as discussed in other chapters of this paper. This assumption has a practical weakness. An agency cannot escape the application and the interpretation of legal rules fixing its own jurisdiction. This very fact may threaten two elements of the conception of a public agency: the limitation of its jurisdiction and the prohibition of its determining its own jurisdiction. It seems to be a vicious circle or a *regressus in infinitum*. This vicious circle can be eliminated by assuming that linguistic convention distinguishes between an agency's *determination* of its own jurisdiction and the *interpretation* of the jurisdiction as determined by other agencies. Professor Kocourek, comparing the jurisdictions of the legislature and the courts, writes that "the court in the last resource is the final authority which determines the limits of this jurisdiction."[57]   I suppose that the expression "final authority"[58] relates to the

[57] *Op. cit.*, p. 106. Sir John Salmond's opinion (*Jurisprudence*, p. 57), "The duty of the final tribunal to administer justice according to law must be recognized as a moral obligation merely," does not apply even to the British legal system. He (*ibid.*) infers the authority of the law over the courts "in the moral obligation of the judges to observe their judicial oaths. . . ." Salmond did not recognize legal rules determining the jurisdiction of courts. Analyzing problems connected with the supreme authority, he explains (*ibid.*, p. 170): "So also the rule that judicial decisions have the force of law is legally ultimate and underived. No statute lays it down."

[58] Final in relation to all people and all agencies except the agency determining this part of the court jurisdiction. The jurisdiction of the federal Supreme Court of the United States is briefly explained by

determination of the meaning of the rules establishing the jurisdiction (competence) of the court. The
fact remains that in each legal system there are one
or more agencies over which there is no legal guardianship except the authority which can change the
constitution itself. This relates as well to legal systems which establish specific courts for supervising
the constitutionality of acts of legislative bodies.

The fact that the authority which has the jurisdiction to change the constitution does not act or
react with reference to a system of interpretation of
the jurisdiction of the supreme tribunal may become
highly significant.[59] The acquiescence[60] of the supreme authority in a broad or specific interpretation
of the legal rules determining the jurisdiction of the
Supreme Court is frequently regarded as a negative
expression of a "will," or as "unwritten" law. It
may be objected that it would be better if the supreme authority did not express its will, tacitly or by
acquiescence, in hotly discussed problems if the constitution itself provides other forms of sign vehicles
for the expression of the will of the supreme authority. Why should political and legal reasoning sup-

Mr. Justice Frankfurter in his article in the *Encyclopaedia of the Social Sciences*, VII, 474 ff.

[59] In the United States the constitutional provisions relating to the
jurisdiction of the Supreme Court were not changed, although such
proposals have been often discussed. See Lauterpacht, *op. cit.*, p. 392.

[60] E. E. McChesnay Sait (*Political Institutions* [New York, 1938],
p. 140) writes about governments operating with the acquiescence of
the people.

plement in such basic and far-reaching questions the clear-cut expression of the will of the authority which is charged with regulating the basic organization of the state? The obstacles which hinder the complete rationalization of a constitution and the operations of the supreme authority—as mentioned above—are of a very complex character. That is why many countries are reluctant to express their constitution in a rationalized form.[61] The difficulties are reflected in many problems of legal practice. Mr. Justice Holmes, recognizing the political importance of these problems, expressed the following opinion: "It seems to me desirable that the work should be done with express recognition of its nature. The time has gone by when law is only an unconscious embodiment of the common will. It has become a conscious reaction upon itself of organized society knowingly seeking to determine its own destinies."[62] He called attention to the fact that "the danger is that such considerations should have their weight in an inarticulate form as unconscious prejudice or half conscious inclination."[63]

The sentences quoted from Mr. Justice Holmes are very significant, emphasizing that a modern legal system has to face the rather involved problem of

[61] See W. S. Holdsworth, *A History of English Law* (Boston, 1926), IX, 7, with reference to the formulation of the prerogatives of the British king.

[62] *Collected Legal Papers*, pp. 129-30. [63] *Ibid.*, p. 129.

the jurisdiction of courts.[64]   He was aware that the more precise *determining* of the jurisdiction of courts does not mean the *narrowing* of it. It is possible, usual, and necessary to delegate to judges power to create specific decisions by applying their opinions pertaining to the moral and social order. It is even possible and usual to empower them to create in this particular way *generally* binding rules,[65] but I do not think that the courts and other public agencies are empowered by super-legal rules to exercise this jurisdiction. If a court acts within the bounds of its jurisdiction, there is not conceivable a "doctrine of judicial absolutism or infallibility," as Morris R. Cohen calls it.[66] Professor Cohen recognized well that finality does not mean infallibility and absolutism.[67] He is right in saying that "To be ruled by a judge is, to the extent that he is not bound by law, tyranny or despotism. It may often be intelligent and benevolent but it is tyranny just the

[64] R. J. Harris writes with regard to some judicial functions: "The federal courts should either abandon this ceremonious pretense or be forced to do so by constitutional amendment." However, such a constitutional amendment would have to be preceded by a positive solution of some important questions of legal and political technique.

[65] J. A. Spruill, Jr. ("The Effect of an Overruling Decision," 18 *N. C. Law Rev.* 204) writes: "We agree with the realists that the courts do legislate. (However, we would stress the fact that they do so subject to rather definite limitations.)"

[66] "A Critical Sketch of Legal Philosophy in America," *Law: A Century of Progress* (New York, 1937), II, 278.

[67] *Ibid.*, and Morris R. Cohen, *Law and the Social Order* (New York, 1933), pp. 207, 212, 213.

same."[68]   Or as Montesquieu put it: "In despotic governments, there are no laws, the judge himself is his own rule."[69]

In by far the majority of cases the men making up a court act according to their prescribed jurisdiction. But they may so act as to overstep consciously or unconsciously the boundaries of their jurisdiction. Such acts are—as pointed out elsewhere —not legal acts, even if they are enforced by the usual law-enforcing machine.[70]   The situation is different if the agency has jurisdiction to create *certain* acts with *finality,* even deviating from the legal rules which have to be applied generally.[71]   It is a question of jurisdiction whether it is empowered to create such acts. Kocourek makes this distinction in another way; he writes: "If a judge decides incorrectly on a question lying within his competence, he exercises an unlawful power of jurisdiction. If a judge decides a case not within his competence, he exercises an unlawful power of non-competence."[72]   The problem of the immunity of judges as to personal

[68] "Positivism and the Limits of Idealism in the Law," 1927 *Columbia Law Rev.* 27, 237, quoted by Kocourek, "Libre recherche in America," *Recueil Gény,* II, 481. Professor Kocourek concurred in the cited opinion of Mr. Cohen.

[69] *Op. cit.,* Book VI, Chap. III.

[70] Cf. Jay Leo Rotschild, "Judicial Immunity for Acts Without Jurisdiction," 7 *Fordh. Law Rev.* 63 ff.

[71] Samuel Williston (*Some Modern Tendencies in the Law* [New York, 1929], p. 51) writes: "Courts themselves have in fact, whether it is acknowledged or not, a still more uncontrolled power to bend a general rule to the needs of the particular case."

[72] *Op. cit.,* p. 325.

responsibility for acting without jurisdiction has to be separated from an analysis of the legality of the acts performed. The jurisdiction of an agency cannot be reconstructed according to the acts which it actually creates or enforces. However, Albert Kocourek assumes that "The ultimate factual supremacy of governmental power lies with whatever agency of government that exercises the power in regular application of the power without successful factual interference by another agency of the same government."[73]

The question whether a court may create or recognize rules of social conduct called general legal rules may be answered—as stated here many times—*only* by taking into account the fact that courts are acting as instruments of the legal order[74] and that there are rules determining the jurisdiction of the particular agency. In connection with the problem of judge-made law the following basic questions may arise: (1) Can (is it conceivable that) an agency have jurisdiction to make a specific decision, even if there are no substantive regulations relating to the case which has to be decided?[75] (2) May individual decisions serve as sign vehicles for general rules of conduct for

[73] *Ibid.*, p. 107.

[74] Harold J. Laski in a recent study about the judicial function emphasizes "the significance of the fact that the judge is an instrument of the State-power."—*The Danger of Being a Gentleman and Other Essays* (New York, 1940), p. 106.

[75] For instance, by giving an agency the jurisdiction over "admiralty and maritime law" cases, or "civil" cases.

people to whom the individual decisions do not apply?[76] (3) If individual decisions of public agencies do not bind people to whom they do not directly apply, as stated in (2), can this general binding force be inferred from other sources than a declaration of the binding force of a legal rule?

The first question asks whether an agency (court) can be enabled to create a specific decision without determining in detail the subject matter of the decision by general or individual (substantive) legal rules; in other words, whether an agency may be directed to decide a case despite the nonexistence of general legal rules with reference to the particular substance of the case. The answer is without any doubt in the affirmative. The problem of "unprovided cases" may be solved by giving a broad jurisdiction to the courts.[77] However, even if the

[76] For instance, by express recognition of the common law *system* by a particular legal system.

[77] For example, Art. 4 of the French Civil Code reads: "A judge refusing to decide a case under the pretext of the silence, obscurity, or insufficiency of the law, should be prosecuted as guilty of the denial of justice." (Art. 1 of the Swiss Civil Code and Art. 7 of the Austrian Civil Code regulate this matter also, but in less severe expressions.) Mitchell Franklin emphasized that "There is no reason to hold that codification precludes judicial inventiveness to eke out situations not dealt with in the code unless the code itself makes unwarranted pretensions to completeness." Mr. Franklin quotes Art. 7 of the Austrian, Art. 4 of the French, and Art. 1 of the Swiss Civil Code, stating that "This is exactly the assumption of these codes."— "Mr. Gény and Juristic Ideals and Method in the United States," *Recueil Gény*, II, 39. John Dickinson took an opposite view in regard to the French Civil Code. Referring to the pertinent literature, he pointed out that the code was considered complete.—"The Problem of the Unprovided Cases," *ibid.*, II, 509 f. It seems to me that the above

jurisdiction-determining rule is seemingly the only rule binding the court, a great many constitutional and other legal rules related indirectly to the case will determine the conduct of the agency. I assume—as mentioned above—that such jurisdiction-conferring rules, according to common usage, imply that, in default of substantial legal rules, the agency has to take account of rule systems of human social conduct with which the particular legal system is necessarily interrelated. The determination of the existence and the choice of such rules implies in itself broad discretion. If such "other" rules are inapplicable, the agency is expected to decide according to principles broadly connoted by the expression "reasonable." Empowering people to decide implies that personal opinions of the deciding persons enter into the process. We know that these personal elements are vigorously influenced by the views of the deciding persons concerning the purpose of the legal order, although the purpose of a rule order transcends its concept in a logical sense. A thoroughgoing analysis of the meaning of enabling a person to decide shows that personal elements are inevitable but limited factors in deciding. In the American literature of the past decades this problem has been

quoted articles of the French, Austrian, and Swiss codes do not support such an assumption with reference to the makers of these codes. See Frederick G. McKean, Jr., "The Law of Laws," 78 *Penna. Law Rev.* 950 ff., and John Dickinson, "Legal Rules: Their Function in the Process of Decision," 79 *Penna. Law Rev.* 834-35.

explained in detail. However, it is one of the most striking features of modern legal systems that, even in matters which are not regulated as to their substance by legal rules, people act with a relative uniformity. Obviously the jurisdiction-determining rule often suffices to predict how the agency would act in case of arising controversies.

The conferring of very broad discretionary powers upon persons is a feature practiced in social life, especially in economic enterprises.[78] Even analogies for personal independence (i.e., the appointment for life) may be easily found. Such persons are expected to act on the one hand according to their initiative, on the other hand according to expressed or implied rules. However, their discretionary powers have not been considered as a *deus ex machina* or from the standpoint of coercive reality alone. The question of discretionary power in other fields has not become veiled with mysticism as it has in the legal field.

The second question asks whether an agency may be enabled to create general rules of conduct as a by-product of individual decisions. This question has to be answered in the affirmative, too.[79] We

[78] See C. E. Merriam, *The Role of Politics in Social Change*, pp. 49 ff.

[79] Blackstone (I *Comm.* 69) on the one hand assumes that judges are not "delegated to pronounce a new law," and states on the other hand that precedents are binding, for they are "the principal and most authoritative evidence" of the common law—except manifestly absurd or unjust decisions; these latter are characterized by Blackstone as "not law" contrasting it with "bad law."

know by experience that individual decisions may
serve as sign vehicles for general legal rules.[80]   It
may be questionable whether the rule enabling the
agency to create general rules by using the sign
vehicle of individual decisions may be called a rule
determining the jurisdiction of the *agency*.   The
meaning of such a jurisdiction-determining rule is
in reality the determination of the conduct of *people*.[81] It is a "regulation by organization."[82] To be
sure, individual decisions of public agencies (even
courts) are not sign vehicles for general legal rules
unless they are so specified.   The expressions "individual rule" or "specific decision" imply that. This
is the answer (from a legal point of view) to the
third question.

It has often been emphasized that general rules
contained in individual decisions may become ex
post facto regulations with reference to factual situations which occurred before the creation of the general rule.[83]   To be sure, it is highly desirable to have
a legal order which avoids ex post facto general
rules, and there are many constitutions prohibiting
or declaring as nonexistent (especially in the field
of criminal law) ex post facto regulations.

[80] See C. K. Allen, *Law in the Making*, pp. 151 ff. Cf. K. N.
Llewellyn, "Case Law," *Encyclopaedia of the Social Sciences*, Vol. III.

[81] See A. S. Beardsley, *op. cit.*, p. 94.

[82] Ernst Freund (*op. cit.*, pp. 78 f.) uses this expression, but not
entirely in the same connection.

[83] See J. A. Spruill, Jr., "The Effect of an Overruling Decision,"
18 *N. C. Law Rev.* 204 ff.

It is significant that such prohibitions are usually applied only to statutory law. Ex post facto regulations may be considered unjust or unsound from the standpoint of a modern legal policy, but this does not change the validity of them if they are covered by the legal system. It is a problem of legal and political technique to reduce ex post facto laws to a minimum.

Whereas the ex post facto character of a general rule may be determined or limited by the authority declaring these rules as generally binding, it seems to be difficult to limit this effect of specific decisions. However, the court may be authorized to avoid hardships resulting from these mere technical difficulties.[84]

We know that individual decisions of public agencies, especially courts, strongly motivate human social conduct, even though the individual decisions are not legally qualified to be sign vehicles for general *legal rules*. Many hundreds of volumes have been written to explain this fact. Napoleon strictly prohibited, in the famous Article 5 of his Code, the adoption of precedents and the creation of general

---

[84] Mr. Justice Cardozo (*The Nature of the Judicial Process*, pp. 146-47) writes: "I say, therefore, that in the vast majority of cases the retrospective effect of judge-made law is felt either to involve no hardship or only such hardship as is inevitable where no rule has been declared. I think it is significant that when the hardship is felt to be too great or to be unnecessary, retrospective operation is withheld."

rules from specific decisions.[85] In this he followed the example of Justinian. It seems evident that in this regard neither of them succeeded.

The legal orders of states throughout the world contribute little to clearing up this problem besides such sentences as contained in the Code Napoléon or in the Code of Justinian[85a] or in some civil codes. Hungary regulated by legal provisions the binding force of the specific decisions of ordinary courts. This is significant, for this state is a country with a so-called unwritten constitution and a law system similar to common law. In Hungary, Statute 54, Articles 70 to 78 (1912), set up regulations governing the binding force of individual decisions of the higher ordinary courts. Another significant example is the Czechoslovakian Statute 164, of June 16, 1937, reforming the organization of the Supreme Administrative Court, which contains in Paragraph 13 provisions relating to *general rules* pertaining to *legal* questions. According to Paragraph 13, such a

[85] "Judges are forbidden when giving judgment in the cases to lay down general rules of conduct or to decide a case by holding it was governed by previous decisions." Cf. Art. 4 of the Japanese statute regulating the administration of justice and the sources of civil law (June 8, 1875), cited by Naojiro Jugiyama, in *Recueil Gény*, II, 446.

[85a] *Code 7, 45, 13:* "De sententiis et interlocutionibus omnium iudicum. . . . Non enim, si quid non bene dirimatur, hoc et in aliorum iudicum vitium extendi oportet, quum *non exemplis, sed legibus iudicandum est.* . . ." (My italics.) However, this principle did not apply to the Decreta of the Emperor, although "Many of them did not more than dispose of the case, but where a new rule of law was laid down or uncertainties cleared up they were binding."—R. W. League and C. H. Ziegler, *Roman Private Law* (London, 1932), p. 15.

general rule may be approved by enlarged chambers of the court and published in the official bulletin of the state as general rules binding the administrative authorities and the ordinary trial chambers of the court as well. The cabinet and the governmental departments have the responsibility of seeing to it that the administrative agencies adapt their conduct to these published general rules. Ordinarily, the questions decided by these general rules come to the surface on the occasion of the court's deciding individual cases, in the event that the ordinary chambers of the court have taken a view deviating from the legal opinion of administrative agencies. It is tacitly understood that such general rules determine the conduct of citizens as well, although they are addressed only to the courts and administrative agencies.

In Switzerland, the first article of the preliminary chapter of the Civil Code regulates this matter: "The law must be applied in all cases which come within the letter or the spirit of any of its provisions. Where no provision is applicable, the judge shall decide according to the existing customary law and, in default thereof, according to the rules which he would lay down if he had himself to act as legislator. Herein he must be guided by approved legal doctrine and case law."[86]

In several other European countries civil codes or

---

[86] *The Swiss Civil Code,* trans. by Ivy Williams (Oxford, 1925), p. 1. Art. 7 of the Austrian Civil Code regulates this matter similarly.

rules governing the internal administration of the courts contain similar provisions. These provisions are especially necessary on the European continent because the higher tribunals operate in several chambers, and there is a danger that the different chambers of the same court would decide similar legal questions differently. In many countries this problem is a play-ball of legal and political doctrine, and a good touchstone for testing the acumen of legal and political scientists.

This is not the place to discuss the American, British, and other doctrines of precedent.[87] However, I would like to refer to one or two characteristic points. Eugene Wambaugh[88] distinguished between imperative authority, persuasive authority,[89] and quasi authority of precedents. He calls them "degrees" of authority. Professor Wambaugh justified the imperative authority of precedents, explaining why a court considers itself imperatively bound by its own decisions and why they are followed by subordinate courts. The last of the reasons which he gives is that by adopting precedents the result of litigations can be predicted and law may become

[87] See Karl Llewellyn, *Präjudizienrecht und Rechtsprechung in Amerika* (Leipzig, 1933), *passim*. Cf. the review of this work by C. J. Friedrich, 50 *Pol. Sc. Quar.* 419 ff., and L. L. Fuller's review in 82 *Penna. Law Rev.* 551.

[88] *The Study of Cases* (Boston, 1894), paragraphs 85-97, pp. 95 f.

[89] Professor Williston uses the expression "only persuasive authority" in evaluating the restatement of the law by the American Law Institute.—*Op. cit.*, p. 101.

certain and safe. According to Wambaugh, "uniformity is essential to law."[90] One could ask whether the "imperative" authority of a precedent is not entirely dependent on the jurisdiction of the court to create general rules. If this aspect is right, the reasons quoted by Professor Wambaugh become important as reasons why the jurisdiction of the court should be determined in a certain manner with reference to the creation of general rules.

Georg Jellinek[91] evolved a doctrine of the regulatory force of factual situations, called "die normative Kraft des Faktischen," which influenced the doctrine of following precedents on the European continent. He tried to explain why men are inclined to infer from a factual situation that because a certain event once happened in a certain manner it ought to happen under similar circumstances that way again. He emphasized that factual situations have the "psychological tendency" to transform themselves into a rule in the normative sense, that is, related to future situations. This feature creates, according to Jellinek, in all legal systems presumptions that an existing *social* situation is a *legal* one and that people who want to change this factual situation have to prove that they have a "better right" to it.[92]

---

[90] *Op. cit.*, p. 97.   [91] *Allgemeine Staatslehre*, pp. 337 ff.

[92] *Ibid.*, pp. 339-40. Morris R. Cohen (*Law and the Social Order*, p. 206) explains why it is so difficult to avoid the confusion between law and custom: ". . . human inertia and imitativeness give custom itself a regulative and normative force, compelling uniformity where the individual might otherwise diverge from the common way. . . ."

Without attempting to review the doctrine of precedents as evolved by great American judges, I would like to reproduce a few sentences from their teachings concerning the limits of the doctrine. "Stare decisis," writes Mr. Justice Brandeis in a dissenting opinion, "is ordinarily a wise rule of action. But it is not a universal, inexorable command."[93] It may be added that a legal rule may declare it a command as well.

Mr. Justice Cardozo taught that, although "conformity is not to be turned into a fetish," the great advantage of following precedents is certainty and uniformity, which "are gains not lightly to be sacrificed."[94]

Mr. Justice Frankfurter said in a recent decision[94a] that "stare decisis embodies an important social policy. It represents an element of continuity in law, and is rooted in the psychologic need to satisfy reasonable expectations. But stare decisis is a principle and not a mechanical formula. . . ." And further, that the American Supreme Court—unlike the British House of Lords—rejected from the beginning "a doctrine of disability at self-correction."

Mr. Justice Holmes writes that "It is revolting to have no better reason for a rule of law than that so

[93] State of Washington vs. Dawson, 264 U. S. 219. Mr. Justice Brandeis emphasized that the precedents which should be overruled "are recent ones. They have not been acquiesced in."

[94] The Paradoxes of Legal Science, pp. 29-30.

[94a] Bryant vs. Helvering, 309 U. S. 106 (1939).

it was laid down in the time of Henry IV. It is still more revolting if the grounds upon which it was laid down have vanished long since, and the rule simply persists from blind imitation of the past."[95] Although Mr. Justice Holmes applied this remark to a particular case,[96] it is fruitful to examine it from a more general point of view. The question remains whether the rule is applied simply from blind imitation of the past, or whether there is a legal rule which revolts people because it does not correspond with their social ideas in reference to what *should* be the legal rule for similar cases. In the latter instance it is a criticism of the legislative authority which does not act according to the wishes of the people. If precedents have binding force upon courts, it is due to the fact that people in general are bound by them. This is the reason why controversies are adjudicated according to them. It seems to be obvious that courts and other public agencies, and even the large masses of people, will be greatly influenced by preceding specific decisions of courts and other public agencies relating to similar factual situations, even if the principles implied in these decisions are not *legally* binding.[97] The difference between the two situations seems to be clear. In the first case

[95] *Collected Legal Papers,* p. 187.

[96] Commonwealth *vs.* Rubin, 165 Mass. 453, *ibid.*

[97] B. A. Wortley (*op. cit.,* p. 24) regards binding precedents as written law and as one of the real and formal sources of law, whereas nonbinding precedents, although written, he considers as a subsidiary source.

the binding force of the specific decisions for similar future cases is determined by a legal rule. In the second case there is no binding force in the legal sense; the "force" of the precedents is given on the one hand by pure reasoning, on the other hand by the fact, which we know from the past, that courts are inclined to act in similar factual situations similarly. Whereas, in the first case noncompliance with the general rules expressed by precedents is an act contrary to the law, in the second case such a deviation cannot be regarded from this point of view.

Lord Justice Slesser, quoting the opinion of Dr. Lévy-Ullman about the difference between the British and continental European legal systems, refers to recent cases (1922, 1927) in which British courts decided according to very ancient precedents. He states that "It is little more than a hundred years since, in the case of *Ashford* v. *Thornton* (1818), that a man was challenged in the courts to ordeal by battle, and the court was compelled to hold that such a right still existed in a challenger." Sir Henry Slesser cites in this connection Lord Ellenborough: "The original law of the land is in favour of wager by battle, and it is our duty to pronounce the law as it is, and not as we may wish it to be. Whatever prejudices, therefore, may justly exist against this mode of trial, still, as it is the law of the land, the Court must pronounce judgment for it."[98]

[98] Sir Henry Slesser, *The Law*, pp. 22-23.

It is obvious that the question whether courts or
other public agencies should be *bound* by precedents
is merely a practical question greatly influenced by
tradition and has to be decided by each particular
legal system.[99]

Arthur Goodhart[100] emphasized that the doctrine
relating to the binding force of precedents has such
a decisive importance that it can furnish a fundamental distinction between the judicial methods in
Great Britain and the other countries of the European continent.[101] This opinion is shared by the
great majority of legal and political scientists. The

[99] See Holland, *op. cit.*, p. 63. "Important parts of almost all subjects, and all, or nearly all, of the law on many subjects is expressed
with binding authority only in the recorded decisions of the courts."—
American Law Institute Proceedings, I, Part 1, 66.

[100] "Le Précédent en droit anglais et continental," *Le Problème
des sources du droit positif* (first report of the International Institute
of Legal Philosophy and Juridical Sociology [Paris, 1934]), p. 39. Dean
Roscoe Pound ("The Theory of Judicial Decision," 36 *Harv. Law Rev.*
643) discussed the differences between the American and French systems in following precedents. A very interesting picture of these differences has been given by A. Kocourek ("Libre recherche in America,"
Recueil Gény, II, 459 ff.). Professor Kocourek, emphasizing that there
is a difference in the degrees of formulatedness between case law and
code law, writes: "This feature of our law gives the appearance of
great uncertainty and instability, but in truth this factor affects essentially only the border lines of the ratio and leaves what lies within
the border lines as a basis of professionally reliable predictions of the
consequences of human conduct." And further: "Without attempting
here to go into the details of Anglo-American judicial practice, it
may be said that the English and American judges are in actual fact
as limited by definitions, classifications, concepts, and rules as is the
continental judge."

[101] H. L. Jolowicz ("Case Law in Roman Egypt," *Journal of the
Society of Public Teachers of Law* [1937], pp. 1-2) tells us that
the newer research in legal history demonstrated that "Romans in
their treatment of decided cases were not unlike the English."

assumption of Mr. Goodhart, especially as it applies to the time period from the last third of the eighteenth century to the first decades of the twentieth century, is well founded.

Those fundamental differences—mentioned by Professor Goodhart—have rapidly diminished, but new differences have become apparent. To be sure, on the European continent extra-judicial doctrine played, and still plays, a more important role in legal and political practice than in Great Britain and in America, as C. K. Allen has stressed in speaking of the French legal system.[102] The legal position and the jurisdiction of courts and the problem of precedents have not been in the *focus* of legal and political discussions as in America.[103] The courts have been discussed on the European continent mainly from the point of view of their "independence" from the executive power, emphasizing that both the judiciary and the executive power are subject to the legislative power.

The prosecution for contempt as a device to enforce obedience to court orders does not exist in the typical European continental legal systems; even

[102] *Op. cit.*, pp. 166 f. With reference to the British system, see A. V. Dicey, *Law and Public Opinion in England* (London, 1936), p. 365.

[103] Goodhart (*op. cit.*, p. 37) assumes that in the United States the examination of the judicial function and its connection with the nature of the law "eclipses" all other questions of legal philosophy by the interest which it presents, to such a point that the traditional analytical method is no longer in favor in English-American literature.

more, this device is little known. The distinction between private and public law has become on the Continent of decisive importance in the distribution and exercising of powers. On the European continent the enforcement of administrative decisions has been conferred upon administrative agencies without court intervention. The adjudication of certain civil controversies and petty offenses by administrative agencies has not been regarded as something extraordinary. A general supervision of coercive acts of administrative agencies by courts—though provided by some constitutions—has been regarded as an ideal which should be gradually attained. However, administrative agencies, even in their adjudicative function, have been subject to obedience to the hierarchically superior executive agencies, whereas courts have been "independent" from such orders. The responsibility of the cabinet for the smooth working of the whole body of public administration implies the principle that its directly and indirectly given orders will be obeyed; i.e., they are presumed to be legal.[104] Non-judicial agencies independent of orders of the executive power exist only in the field of auditing public debts and for similar purposes.

In the second half of the nineteenth century a

[104] Walter Jellinek (*Verwaltungsrecht*, p. 268) stressed in his discussion of invalid administrative acts the doctrine that "an administrative act—however deficient—in case of doubt is to be regarded as valid." On page 313 he tries to destroy the illusion of faithful citizens "that there is a *general* supervision of administrative acts by courts."

mighty political movement sprang up on the Continent as a result of the growing belief that a legal order (in order to be legal) has to provide for the possibility of review of all acts which pretend to derive their force from the legal order. This movement was directly responsible for setting up in its various forms the system of administrative courts. The French Council of State and the Austrian Supreme Administrative Court represented the main types of these new courts. The Council of State in Paris succeeded in gradually building up a doctrine that nearly all acts of the executive power are subject to supervision by independent courts. However, this doctrine—like the main parts of the French administrative procedure—has been based upon "judge-made law." I quote the significant advice given by Professor Louis Roland to students of French administrative law: "It is absolutely impossible to study seriously French administrative law without consulting judicial decisions, especially those of the Council of State."[105] It is not necessary to stress the fact that the British and American doctrine had regarded judicial review of executive acts as a requirement of a legal system, when in continental Europe it was only a political ideal. Thus Felix Frankfurter and James M. Landis could rightly say in the preface to their book, *The Business of the Supreme Court,* "To an extraordinary degree legal

[105] *Précis de droit administratif,* p. 14.

thinking dominates the United States," and further, ". . . no other country in the world leaves to the judiciary the powers which it exercises over us."[106] To explain the reasons for these various developments would require an analysis of the political position of European continental countries. The political stability enjoyed by Great Britain and America for a long time allowed them to maintain a political system which approached perfection, whereas the political insecurity both within and without many countries on the Continent did not make it advisable for those governments to expose the executive power to the light of judicial review. The reviewer of the role of the courts in different legal systems will have to take into account the radical turn in the conception and regulation of the independence of the courts and the turn against the supervision of administrative acts by courts caused by the *new* European revolution.[107]

It has been mentioned before that the focusing of the legal doctrine upon the function of courts is significant for some American legal and political doctrines.[108] These doctrines apply only to "courts"

[106] (New York, 1928), p. v.

[107] Walter Jellinek characterizes this movement as a *backturn* (Rückbau) and designates it as the most important change in the evolution of administrative law.—Supplement to his *Verwaltungsrecht* (Berlin, 1934), p. 17.

[108] A comprehensive presentation of these doctrines is given by A. Kocourek in his paper, "Libre recherche in America," *Recueil Gény,* II, 459 ff. Karl N. Llewellyn, discussing the problems of recent jurisprudence, has been concentrating his attention on the jurisdiction and

in the British and American sense. That is why Mr. Jerome Frank would agree that his conception of "law" and "court law" relates only to countries with a court system in the American sense.[109] These doctrines do not take into account to a sufficient degree the fact that a great many legal provisions are obeyed for many decades without being interpreted by the courts. Eugen Ehrlich, stressing that "in general only the decisions of the highest and most respected courts create legal provisions," called attention to the "affairs" which "work themselves out without any dispute."[110] However, Professor Ehr-

operation of courts, especially the problem of the predictability of court decisions.—"On Reading and Using the Newer Jurisprudence," 40 *Col. Law Rev.* 581 ff. See J. L. Kunz, *op. cit.,* pp. 377-78 (note 13); see especially his discussion of the "legal" position of the judge.

[109] *Law and the Modern Mind,* p. 47. Mr. Frank openly admitted that in his book the emphasis "on the conduct of judges is admittedly artificial." He stressed that "the law" considered in this book is "court-law." Professor Joseph W. Bingham emphasized that his article, "What is Law" (11 *Mich. Law Rev.* 1, 109), relates to the system of jurisprudence which prevails in the English speaking part of the world (p. 121, footnote 38). Gerhard Husserl ("Everyday Life and the Law," 5 *Social Philosophy* 324) writes: "Law is what the judge dispenses." Law intervenes, according to Husserl, "when frictions have arisen in the social sphere which transcend the happenings of everyday life."—*Ibid.,* p. 311.

[110] "The Sociology of Law," 36 *Harv. Law Rev.* 141. "Judicial decisions," writes Dr. Ehrlich, "flow only from those cases which are brought before the court. . . . But only very few matters come before the court. Most affairs work themselves out without any dispute. There are unnumbered persons who stand or have stood innumerable legal relations without ever having anything to do with courts or officers. In general only the decisions of the highest and most re- .spected courts create Legal Provisions, and inasmuch as many kinds of disputes in which only negligible sums are involved never reach these courts, it comes about that *there are no Legal Provisions for them.* . . . Finally, it must be borne in mind that Legal Provisions are naturally *lacking for new legal situations* because it necessarily

lich's explanation should be read in connection with his assumption that "A legal provision is an instruction framed in words addressed to courts as to how to decide legal cases (Entscheidungsnorm) or a similar instruction addressed to administrative officials as to how to deal with particular cases (Verwaltungsnorm)."[111] Professor Ehrlich distinguished

takes some time until a sufficient number of legal disputes involving them reach the point of judicial decision and until they are forced upon the attention of juristic writers." (My italics.) Fortunately people comply with legal rules without waiting upon their recognition by courts, although, if and when they become interpreted by courts, people generally adopt the meaning of the rules as interpreted. Thurman W. Arnold recommends a specific policy in order to create precedents spelling out the broad purposes of the Sherman Act. Such precedents should determine the policy of prosecuting antitrust cases.— *The Bottlenecks of Business* (New York, 1940), p. 171.

[111] "The Sociology of Law," 36 *Harv. Law Rev.* 132. Karl N. Llewellyn wrote in *The Bramble Bush* (pp. 3, 11) the frequently cited sentences: "What these officials do about disputes is, to my mind, the law itself. . . . And that the rules of law are important in so far as they give us a guide to what the officials will do or how we can get them to do something." Professor Llewellyn tells us that these cited sentences have to be "taken in conjunction with Chapter V of that book," and even then he regards the "emphasis as out of balance."— "On Reading and Using the Newer Jurisprudence," 40 *Col. Law. Rev.* 603n. The quoted study of Mr. Llewellyn eliminated several misunderstandings in this connection. Dr. Pound writes in his *Contemporary Juristic Theory* (p. 15): "In the policy of the English-speaking world, law was taken to govern official action. Now we are told that the law is whatever is done officially." See L. L. Fuller, "American Legal Realism," 82 *Penna. Law Rev.* 429 ff. It should be mentioned in this connection that one of the founders of modern administrative law on the European continent, Otto Mayer (*Deutsches Verwaltungsrecht*, I, 84 ff.), assumed that the relationship of public officials to their higher authorities is based upon force ("Gewaltverhältnis") as contrasted to a relationship based upon law. The same construction is applied by Otto Mayer (*ibid.*, pp. 9-10) to the commands of the military authorities. Llewellyn is concerned with official behavior, with the interaction between official behavior and laymen's behavior, with the recognition of official behavior, and with the behavior of people

legal *norms* ("the legal command, reduced to practice, as it obtains in a definite association . . . even
without any formulation in words") from legal
propositions ("the precise, universally binding formulation of the legal precept in a book of statutes
or in a law book").[112]

It would be too far afield to treat the problem

who "make up" the official's authority, even in discussing "Laymen's
Behavior as a Part of the Law," in "Realistic Jurisprudence—The
Next Step," 30 *Col. Law Rev.* 457. I assume that this doctrine should
be viewed—as far as the layman is concerned—from the angle of his
statement that ordinary people or laymen adopt as the bases of their
conduct not legal norms but social norms ("gesellschaftliche Normen").
According to Llewellyn these two norms often coincide.—*Präjudizienrecht,* pp. 81-82. Edwin W. Patterson ("A Required Course in Jurisprudence," 9 *Amer. Law School Rev.* 589), suggesting the outlines of
a course in jurisprudence, discussed the ways of teaching "What is
Law," among other points of the subject matter. He considers the
giving of a definition of "a law which satisfies the requirements of
the analytical school. The problems here are," according to Professor
Patterson, "to separate legal norms from other norms, and to note
the competing theory that the law is what officials do." Albert Kocourek finishes his study ("Libre recherche in America," *Recueil Gény,*
II, 459 ff.) with the following sentences: "The free judge movement
attempts to make a virtue of uncertainty in the law. . . . It puts all
the emphasis upon an ultimate realism, even when the ultimate fact
is the product of mistake or even prejudice or corruption. That extreme point of view furnishes nothing for a legal science even though
it places in clear relief the actual forces which enter into the judicial
process" (p. 497). I assume that the main problem is whether or not
the concept of "public officials" implies the following essential elements: physical persons who perform acts according to their jurisdiction as determined (and essentially limited) by legal rules; the
appointment of such persons by other physical persons whose jurisdiction is to make such appointments; the performance of legal acts
by public officials; a general understanding about the verification of
acts, whether they are legal or nonlegal. It has been discussed above
that such a general understanding may be attained to a high degree
but not with an absolute certainty.

[112] *Principles of the Sociology of Law,* p. 38. With reference to
Ehrlich's distinction between "state law" and "living law," see Max
Rheinstein, 48 *Inter. Journ. of Ethics* 237.

of the concept of the legal rule as it centers on the behavior of courts and public officials with reference to the totalitarian system of government. It would be even more vain to discuss here the revived institutions called "political courts," which, according to renewed political doctrines, have been designed to eliminate political adversaries of the regime in the disguise of a "judicial" process.

I conclude that the concept of a legal system implies a legal machine which, according to legal rules determining its jurisdiction, is in a position to review the legality of acts which pretend to be regarded as legal. This machine is usually a court system.[113] H. Lauterpacht states that "Whatever may be the nature of such rules the very fact that there are no impartial tribunals to adjudicate upon their operation seriously impairs their character as rules of law."[114] It is a matter of convenience whether the same or different agencies review acts of private persons stated to be in accordance with the legal order and acts of public agencies other than courts. Similarly, it is a question which may be decided by the particular legal order, whether or not the individual decisions of certain courts should have a general binding force.

[113] Including administrative courts in the European continental sense, and even military courts if they are endowed by the necessary "independence."

[114] *Op. cit.,* p. 424. Lauterpacht (*ibid.,* footnote 1) registers the opinion of Bluntschli "that the absence of the judge is even more serious than the absence of a legislator." It would be vain to object that the legislator has to determine the jurisdiction of courts.

VI

LEGAL SECURITY

ALTHOUGH WE KNOW by immediate evidence that
the properties of security, certainty, and predictability are inherent in what we call a "legal system,"
today it is sometimes questioned whether legal systems are, or may be, secure and certain and whether
the consequences of legal rules are, or may be, generally predictable. Witnessing the breakdown of
international and national political systems and institutions and the stripping bare of deeply rooted
legal and political doctrines, one must question
whether it is timely just now to discuss such problems as security, certainty, and predictability in connection with legal systems. Will not security pass
from the political picture for the next several decades, permitting new political dynamics of insecurity
to work? Such a famous philosopher as A. N.
Whitehead, in his *Science and the Modern World,*
wrote: "The middle-class pessimism over the future
of the world comes from a confusion between civilization and security. In the immediate future there
will be less security than in the immediate past, less
stability. It must be admitted that there is a degree

of instability which is inconsistent with civilization. But on the whole, the great ages have been unstable ages."[1] Whitehead admitted freely that a degree of stability is a requisite of human civilization; he admitted also that stability in this particular sense may be expressed in degrees. However, it is interesting to analyze the parallelism between stability and security with reference to a *legal* order.

Legal security seems to be a prerequisite for living as a political unit, for legal security is today the basis for social security. Legal security is not a postulate desired only by the man in the street; it is generally recognized that it represents the interests of both the community and the individual citizens. The attack on political and legal techniques which aim to increase legal security is frequently a concealed attack against certain institutions which are established by the legal order. A famous antagonist of democratic government, Nicolas Berdyaev, in his well-known book, *The End of Our Time,*[2] described the present upheaval in Europe as "in reality directed against the foundations of modern history, against unsubstantial liberalism, against individualism, against juridical formalism." It is certainly true that juridical formalism is attacked as maintaining the essential rigidity of legal orders, and it is in a certain sense an ironical synonym for legal security.

[1] (Penguin edition, London, 1938), pp. 240-41.
[2] (London, 1934), p. 144.

Legal security is only one of several possible aspects from which we can measure and view a legal order. A highly secure legal order may become obnoxious and disastrous for the people of a country by reasons which lie on other levels. Thus we have to be aware that in analyzing legal security we do not regard the legal rules from a synoptic viewpoint; i.e., we question only *how* they are determining social relations.

It has been objected that certainty, security, and predictability in connection with a legal order are empty and misleading words, having whatever significance they might have merely in degree. It has been questioned whether such phenomena as legal rules represent may become verifiable at all. And even with reference to an immediate impression of what people regard as most certain, it has been stated "that this absolute certainty is restricted to events of a private world only. With the transition from my own subjective experience to the objective external world, uncertainty enters into my statements. But not only uncertainty as to special statements; there is superimposed a general uncertainty as to the world of external things at all."[3]

[3] H. Reichenbach, *op. cit.*, p. 90. "The quest for certainty," writes John Dewey, "by means of exact possession in mind of immutable reality is exchanged for search for security by means of active control of the changing course of events."—*The Quest for Certainty, A Study of the Relation of Knowledge and Action* (New York, 1928), p. 204. With reference to the problem of absolute certainty, see Edmund Husserl, *Ideen zu einer reinen Phänomenologie und phänomenologischen Philosophie* (Halle a. d. S., 1928), p. 86.

Even natural sciences have in the last few decades modestly substituted for their proud terms, "truth," "certainty," and "predictability," such humbler expressions as "statistical truth," "relative certainty," and "probability." I agree with the objectors as far as they connect truth, security, certainty, and predictability in one of their particular meanings with supernatural sciences or with immediate personal impressions, and I admit that all these terms express only degrees in this connection. Political and legal sciences, in accordance with common usage, employ these terms to express relatively high degrees of security, certainty, and predictability. Exactness and finality in the severe sense that they were used formerly by natural sciences do not apply to these terms as they are conceived in legal and political sciences. H. Reichenbach, stating, generally, that "Knowledge is an approximative system which will never become 'true,'" called attention to the fact that "It is one of the elementary laws of approximative procedure that the consequences drawn from a schematized conception do not hold outside the limits of the approximation."[4]

The political and human significance of "perfectly" certain and predictable legal rules was illus-

[4] *Op. cit.*, p. vi. "There is no certainty at all remaining," writes Reichenbach, "all that we know can be maintained with probability only. There is no Archimedean point of absolute certainty left to which to attach our knowledge of the world; all we have is an elastic net of probability connections floating in open space."—*Ibid.*, p. 192.

trated in a striking manner by Shakespeare in the trial of Shylock *vs*. Antonio, the Merchant of Venice. Political and legal scientists have often quoted both sides of the Shakespearean moral:

First, the strictly verbal application of the legal institution of contracts enabling Shylock to cut out a pound of the poor merchant's flesh, and second, the reversal of the rule against Shylock by interpreting the law in an unexpected manner.

Who knows whether the genius of Shakespeare could have predicted that European countries would present to political and legal history twentieth-century cases which surpass in sophistry and cruelty the classical trial of Venice?

In order to discuss legal security as a possible element or as a necessary property of a legal system, it may be profitable to sketch a workable concept of a legal system, emphasizing that this concept does not claim to define in an exact manner what is called a legal system. It is superfluous to state that from other viewpoints there may be described other concepts of the terms legal system and legal rules. The conception as described below attempts to give a foundation to a brief and very fragmentary discussion of the proposition that legal security—implying legal certainty and legal predictability—is an essential element of a legal system.

I assume that what is today called a legal system is a combination of many social facts directly and indirectly attributed to a self-centered social entity called an independent *state*. As discussed above, the reverse is not necessarily true; what is called an independent state may be organized on another basis from that which is termed in this paper a legal system. In the process of time a legal system and a state are regarded as—and are intended to be— *durable* institutions established and maintained for an *indefinite* time period. In spatial relation the legal system and the state are connected with *determined land area,* including more or less precisely determined parts of the sea and of the air-space. The state and the legal system refer to a *greater number of people* connected by the existence of their state and the legal system. However, they are connected also by other coexistent rule systems influencing their social behavior, and these "other" rule systems are essentially interactive with the legal system. The connection of people by a legal system in a social organism called state implies the existence of a *common political will* of the people (or a great majority of them) in co-operation in the political form of this particular system. The concept of a legal system implies the recognition of the individual as a social, political, or economic entity. From this it may be inferred that an individual may obtain from an appropriate agency review of acts which are presented as legal. The state and the legal system are related in many dimensions to other states and legal systems which coexist in the process of time. However, the very existence of the legal system and of an independent state implies actual or potential *force* to maintain the state and the legal system by physical strength if necessary, even against the opposing will, if any, of another social entity. A legal system is composed of a set of interrelated (regularly in a human language) manifested sentences, determining human social conduct. These sentences are virtually established, maintained, and changed by human volition; they are generally knowable and generally complied with, though they are essentially enforceable. The concept of the legal system implies the existence of organized "legal" institutions based upon legal rules. That legal security is an essential element of a legal order is implied by the fact that it is a durable social institution, having as subject matter social co-operation, and the fact that it is established for a large number of people. Legal security is further implied by the facts of the interrelationship of legal rules and of the general compliance of people with them.

The third session of the Institute Internationale of Legal Philosophy and Juridical Sociology discussed the topic: Purposes of the Law: Common Good, Justice, Security. The prevailing number of the participants in the discussion did not make a clear distinction between legal security and social (or general) security. Some of the debaters supposed that the topic, Common Good, Justice, and Legal Security as the end of the law, was the subject of their session. One brief remark of Julius Moor[5] called attention to this fundamental distinction, without making the impression which it deserved. Even Dr. Moor's concept that legal security expresses only the validity of the law did not exhaust the meaning of legal security according to common usage.

Legal security has been generally discussed often

[5] *Report of the Institute* . . . *1937-38* (Paris, 1938), p. 60. Professor Moor, discussing the reports of Gustav Radbruch and J. T. Delos, objected that both of them regarded the end of the law as indicated by the alternative of common good and justice on the one hand, and legal security on the other. He asserted that the end of the law transcends the concept of the law and cannot be immanent in it. Therefore, since legal security is immanent in the law, it cannot be regarded as one of the ends or the end of the law. Dr. Moor objected to the identification of legal security with the legal order by Delos, and also objected to Radbruch's interpretation of legal security as the certitude of the vigor of the law. According to Mr. Moor, legal security is immanent in the law, for it expresses only the validity of the law (positive law). In the literature, as attested by Mr. Moor, one uses the term legal security for two concepts which both signify "the real validity of the law." On the one hand, legal security signifies the certitude, as a property of the law, that the law will be applied, and on the other hand it signifies the *jus strictum,* a "system where the legal reality is predetermined by a system of general rules and where as a consequence of this predetermination those who apply the law do not have the faculty at all to shape the legal reality." See J. L. Kunz, *op. cit.,* p. 381. Gustav Radbruch ("La sécurité en droit d'après la théorie anglaise," 6 *Archives de philosophie du droit et de sociologie juridique* [Cahier double, 3-4], pp. 86 ff.) discusses especially the doctrines concerning legal security of Francis Bacon, Frederick Pollock, Dicey, Goodhart, Maine, John Selden, Coke, Blackstone, Hobbes, Hale, and Bentham. He quotes (p. 93) the pertaining characteristic sentence of F. Bacon: "Legis tantum interest ut certa est, ut absque hoc nec justa esse possit."

under several headings. Many authors have examined it in connection with social security. One or two examples may demonstrate this. John Stuart Mill, discussing the connection between Justice and Utility,[6] examined the meaning of having a right "which society ought to defend me in the possession of." The interest involved in this institution is—according to John Stuart Mill—"that of security, to every one's feelings the most vital of all interests." He estimated security as a very important social requirement, saying, "All other earthly benefits are needed by one person, not needed by another; and many of them can, if necessary, be cheerfully foregone, or replaced by something else, but security no human being can possibly do without; on it we depend for all our immunity from evil, and for the whole value of all and every good, beyond the passing moment; since nothing but the gratification of the instant could be of any worth to us, if we could be deprived of anything the next instant by whoever was momentarily stronger than ourselves." John Stuart Mill emphasized that security can be maintained only if "the machinery for providing it is kept unintermittently in active play." He assumes "that the difference in degree (as is often the case in psychology) becomes a real difference in kind."

Another famous representative of Utilitarianism, Jeremy Bentham, discussed "Security" in Chapters

[6] *Utilitarianism, Liberty, and Representative Government,* p. 50.

VII-XIII of the "Objects of the Civil Law," in his *Principles of the Civil Code.* He introduced these chapters by saying, "We have now arrived at the principal object of the Laws: the care of security. This inestimable good is the distinctive work of civilization: it is entirely the work of the laws. Without law there is no security; consequently no abundance. . . ." Bentham, emphasizing the economic importance of security, regarded it as "always tottering, always threatened [in war] when the laws which gave security are suspended." That is why "It requires in the legislator, vigilance continually sustained." Jeremy Bentham recognized well the implications of his opinion with reference to the institution of private property. He designated the opinion of Beccaria ("The right of property is a terrible right, and may not perhaps be necessary") as a "doubt subversive of the social order" (Chap. IX). Bentham, in stating the objections which could arise against his concept of security with reference to the public interest, enumerated six limitations as "sacrifices of security to security" (Chap. XIII), and made a distinction between "the ideal perfection of security, and that perfection which is practicable." The principles of security and equality were regarded by him as "up to a certain point incompatible," but with a little patience and skill they might be brought by degrees to coincide (Chap. XII). Bentham presumed that economic prosperity would lead necessarily towards economic equality if there were no entails, nor monopolies, and if there were no restraint of trade nor restraint of exchange. He was not particularly in favor of ideas propagating "the community of goods," opining that the "cry for equality is only a pretext to cover the robbery which idleness perpetrates upon industry. . . . The establishment of equality is a chimera: the only thing which can be done is to diminish inequality" (Chap. XI). Bentham attempted to reconcile the principle of the greatest possible happiness of the greatest possible number with his concept of social security. He indicated, with an understandable timidity, on the one hand that security does not imply a complete social stability, and on the other hand that there must be "sacrifices of security to security." Obviously, he foresaw the conflicts to come if people would connect the notion of security with the content of a desired social or legal order.

Among the recent scholars I refer only to René Demogue, who discussed "Security" and "Evolution and Security" in Chapters XIII and XIV of his *Fundamental Notions of Private Law,* the first part of which has been translated into English.[7] Demogue regarded the need for security as "the most important of the desiderata of social and legal life, its central motor." Like John Stuart Mill and Ben-

[7] *Modern French Legal Philosophy,* trans. by Mrs. Franklin W. Scott and Joseph P. Chamberlain (Modern Legal Philosophy Series, New York, 1921).

tham, he did not make a conspicuous distinction between social and legal security. Under the heading, "Other Interpretations of Security,"[8] Demogue discusses how "To safeguard security in legal relations. . . ." He analyzed nearly all actual phases of the problem and called attention to the misconception of security as opposing social and political progress. Demogue considered "perfect security as unattainable and undesirable"[9] and recommended dynamic security as a realizable aim of a legal order. Quoting Edward Lambert, he writes: "Perfect security would require the infinite immobility of society,"[10] to which Mr. Justice Cardozo has added that "perfect certainty would mean the same."[11]

In America a rather sharp discussion has been taking place about important aspects of legal security, legal certainty, and legal predictability. The extent and the purport of the discussion is significant because it shows that in such a rapidly developing social and economic order an adequate legal system is being sought. In this connection one should refer to C. K. Allen's explanation of the "immediate occasion" of the American so-called

[8] *Ibid.*, pp. 421-25.   [9] *Ibid.*, p. 444.   [10] *Ibid.*, p. 445.
[11] *The Paradoxes of Legal Science*, p. 6. Mr. Justice Cardozo emphasized that in his essay about Rest and Motion he is concerned "with the law as it is shaped by the judicial process." That is why he taught: "If we figure stability and progress as opposite poles, then at one pole we have the maxim of stare decisis and the method of decision by the tool of a deductive logic; and on the other we have the method which subordinates origins to its end."

"relativistic legal philosophy."[12] Recognizing the great achievements of the American legal system, he suggests that the immediate occasion for the above-mentioned relativistic legal philosophy "has been the extraordinarily complex legal situation which exists in America." According to Allen, in England "the ascertainment and application of 'authority' does not present the same practical difficulties as in America, though, as we shall see, these difficulties are growing."[13] In my opinion the legal situation which exists in America is not more complicated than that in European countries. The difference is that in America certain practical problems of vital importance have been discussed with a greater intensity, whereas in European countries such problems have often remained in the background of political and legal discussion.[14]

The most valuable contribution to the problem of legal security from the theoretical and technical points of view was made by two great American

[12] *Op. cit.*, p. 42.   [13] *Ibid.*, pp. 42-43.
[14] Walter Bagehot discussed many years ago American realism as "the prosaic turn of mind" in the "new communities," as he called America, Australia, and New Zealand. "In the American mind and in the colonial mind there is, as contrasted with the old English mind, a *literalness,* a tendency to say, 'The facts are so-and-so, whatever may be thought or fancied about them. . . .' Physical difficulty is the enemy of early communities, and an incessant conflict with it for generations leaves a mark of reality on the mind—a painful mark almost to us, used to impalpable fears and the half-fanciful dangers of an old and complicated society. The 'new Englands' of all latitudes are bare minded (if I may so say) as compared with the 'old.'"— In the chapter, "Checks and Balances," *The English Constitution* (London, Oxford Press, 1933), p. 223.

judges. O. W. Holmes, Jr., and B. N. Cardozo discussed in many of their writings legal security, legal certainty, and legal predictability in all of their legal, economic, and political implications. They showed us both the necessity and the limits of legal security in a modern and progressive legal order.

While some jurists are fighting in the literary field over whether or not there is a certainty in the legal order, other jurists are doing considerable work in technically improving the degree of legal security, legal certainty, and legal predictability. It is not paradoxical to state that even scholars who maintained that the effort to attain a high degree of legal certainty is fruitless have contributed a great deal to clarify the present situation by bringing it more sharply to the fore.[15]

The term "certainty" means in a *legal* sense that there is an adequate perceivableness of the legal rules and that a relatively high number of people whose social conduct is directly and indirectly determined by the legal order and who have the mental faculties to perceive the pertinent legal rules should have an opportunity to learn them.[16] The concept

[15] For the work done by Jerome Frank, see Karl N. Llewellyn, "Using the Newer Jurisprudence," 40 *Col. Law Rev.* 598.

[16] Cf. Benjamin N. Cardozo, *The Growth of the Law*, pp. 1 ff., and the *Proceedings of the First [Organization] Meeting of the American Law Institute*, I, Part 2, 66 ff., "The Law's Uncertainty and Complexity." With reference to legal technique, see Courtenay Gilbert, *The Mechanics of Law-Making* (New York, 1914), *passim*. There is a comprehensive discussion of the problem of legal security and predictability and, in this framework, of legal certainty in Karl N.

of certainty would suppose on the one hand that
everybody whose conduct is determined by the rule
and who is interested in this conduct knows the
adequately perceivable sign vehicle of the rules, and
on the other hand that the meaning of the sign vehicle is in the process of time the same for everybody. We know that, unfortunately, both requirements are practically unattainable. That is why we
have to reduce the requirements for "legal certainty"
briefly to the following points: (1) The sign vehicle
of the legal rules should have a structure which will
allow a close approach to the attainment of the ideal
of certainty, and (2) legal and political technique
should attain a level which makes possible the ascer-
tainability of legal rules. It is obvious that if general
legal rules provide facts (measures) according to
which individual legal rules (specific decisions) may
be brought into being in the future, such facts
should be made knowable as well. We know that
rather large legal areas are determined either by
allotting a jurisdiction to an agency[17] or by referring
people in the case of disputes to the decision of an
agency. In such cases legal certainty will be limited
to the knowability of the jurisdiction-determining
legal rules and to certain facts according to which

Llewellyn, *Präjudizienrecht*, Part I, par. 52-61. Llewellyn significantly
distinguishes (par. 57-58) between legal security as necessary for the
lawyer and security as required for ordinary people.

[17] As discussed above, the problem of unprovided cases is often
regarded as solved in this manner.

the agencies are expected to decide. This point is a limit for legal certainty which cannot be solved—only reduced—by legal technique. Even scholars representing the opinion called the declaratory theory of law have to admit that in such cases only the rules conferring jurisdiction and the facts determined by legal rules which serve as measures for the exercising of the discretionary power are all that can be made certain. A. Kocourek examined not only the reasons for legal uncertainty but pointed out what should be done in order to reduce it.[18] According to him, "it by no means follows that the ideal situation may not be measurably approached, or that the effort is beyond human power."

The legal certainty of the so-called statutory law approaches in many regards the physical certainty as to the existence of sign vehicles to whose existence there is no objection. The certainty is lessened practically only by the possibility that they do not correspond to the constitutional requirements which determine their creation or their maintenance and by the inevitable occurrence of several meanings of a sign vehicle.[19] The legal certainty of case law depends upon several circumstances. One may question which of many decisions and which parts of specific decisions are sign vehicles for rules of gen-

---

[18] *Op. cit.*, pp. 173-85.
[19] Frederick J. De Sloovère ("Textual Interpretation of Statutes," 11 *N. Y. U. Law Quar. Rev.* 541) discusses certainty and predictability in this connection.

eral application. If there are several decisions pertaining to similar factual situations, the ascertaining of the required human conduct may become very difficult. However, when a rule of general applicability is expressed in an individual decision, it may have the advantage of being more easily understood with reference to particular factual situations. The advantages and desirable limitations of the system of following precedents have been often discussed from the viewpoint of legal security. The development of modern legal systems shows that the case law in its ancient structure is gradually being recognized by statutory law as its complement in order to fill out its deficiencies.[20]

Predictability in the legal sense means very broadly the ability to determine in advance what will happen in the future as a direct or indirect consequence of legally relevant factual situations. In an extreme sense, one could include foretelling what general legal rules will be created in the future as a direct or indirect consequence of past or future factual situations, how people will interpret legal rules, whether or not people will comply with them, and whether and how legal rules will be enforced in the event of their not being complied with. Common usage applies the term predictability in connection with the legal order in a narrower sense. This narrower sense applies to predictions as to how *public*

[20] E. Freund, *op. cit.*, p. 13.

agencies[21] will react as a consequence of existing or future legally relevant factual situations; that is, whether those agencies will react toward a factual situation in the past, present, or future, and, if they do, how they will react.

Such a questioning presupposes the given jurisdiction of certain rule-determining agencies. The rules determining the jurisdiction of an agency are not subject to prediction but should be certain in order to predict how the agency will act or react. But we cannot avoid predictions pertaining to the interpretation of rules determining the jurisdiction of the agency.

A workable doctrine of legal predictability depends upon the results of the science of general predictability of human conduct.[22] The problem of whether human social conduct as a process in time is predictable has greatly concerned political and legal scientists and other scholars far back to early

---

[21] Dr. Roscoe Pound ("Individualization of Justice," 7 *Fordh. Law Rev.* 159) discussed the differences between security and predictability in the judicial process on the one side and in the administrative process on the other side.

[22] Reichenbach (*op. cit.*, p. 75) writes: "It has been the fate of the positivistic doctrines that they have been driven by logical criticism into an intellectual asceticism which has suppressed all understanding of the 'bridging' task of science—the task of constructing a bridge from the known to the unknown, from the past to the future. The cause for this unhealthy doctrinarianism is to be found in underestimating the concept of probability. Probability is not an invention made for the sport of gamblers, or for the business of social statistics, it is the essential form of every judgment concerning the future and the *representative* of truth for any case where *absolute* truth cannot be obtained."

ages. Bishop Jeremy Taylor elucidated in the seventeenth century the Jesuit doctrine in this relation.[23] Leibnitz proposed the application of the concept of mathematical expectation to jurisprudence.[24] David Hume wrote in his famous essay, "That Politics May Be Reduced to Science," the following rather optimistic opinion: "So great is the force of laws and of particular forms of government, and so little dependence have they on the humours and tempers of men, that consequences almost as general and certain may sometimes be deduced from them, as any which the mathematical sciences afford us."[25] P. S. Laplace wrote about unlimited determinism,[26] and gave the famous formulation of the ratio of the favorable cases to the possible cases, valid under the controversial presupposition of "equally possible" cases.[27] S. D. Poisson, the celebrated French mathematician, published a scholarly work, *Recherches sur la probabilité des jugements en matière criminelle et en matière civile.*[28]

Today many scholars are concerned with the study

[23] J. M. Keynes, *A Treatise on Probability* (London, 1921), p. 308.
[24] *Ibid.* The juristic work of Leibnitz has been often discussed. See Gustav Hartmann, "Leibnitz als Jurist und Rechtsphilosoph," in *Festgabe der Juristenfakultät zu Tübingen für Rudolf von Ihering* (Tübingen, 1892).
[25] *Essays Moral, Political, and Literary,* ed. by T. H. Green and T. H. Grose (London, 1898), I, 99.
[26] See Richard von Mises, *Probability, Statistics, and Truth* (New York, 1939), p. 313. The limits of the new probability doctrines have been examined by André Weil, "Calcul des probabilités, méthode axiomatique, intégration," 78 *Revue Scientifique,* 201 ff.
[27] Reichenbach, *op. cit.,* p. 301.   [28] Paris, Bachelier, 1837.

of the predictional value of past and present facts related to human conduct in the future.[29] The result of these studies is significant for legal predictions too. The legislator, the economist, the man in the street, consciously and unconsciously act according to some of these scientifically determined predictional values and according to subjective expectations based upon experience and upon irrational feeling. "Actions demand a decision about unknown events; with our attempt to make this decision as favorable as possible the application of probability statements becomes unavoidable."[30] The "rational degree" of expectation depends upon the frequency of occurrence of similar facts, whether the legally relevant situation is a "typical" one, whether it is connected with actual political issues, and so on. Reichenbach, discussing the problem of "the applicability of the frequency interpretation to the single case," writes: "Thus although the individual event remains unknown, we do best to believe in the occurrence of the most probable event as determined by the frequency interpretation; in spite of possible failures, this principle will lead us to the best ratio of successes which is attainable."[31] It depends a great deal upon the extension of the time period between the

[29] Cf. J. M. Keynes, *op. cit.*, pp. 307 ff., and Reichenbach, *op. cit.*, p. 302.

[30] Reichenbach, *op. cit.*, p. 309. Cf. Jerome Frank, "What Courts Do in Fact," 26 *Ill. Law Rev.* 645 ff., 761 ff., and "Are Judges Human?" 80 *Penna. Law Rev.* 17 ff., 233 ff.

[31] *Op. cit.*, pp. 309-10.

formulation of the expectation and the time for which the prediction is to be made. The mere fact that the final decision of a dispute may take several years greatly complicates the induction of how the case may be decided.

Obviously, legal certainty and legal predictability are very closely related to each other, and the concept of predictability widely overlaps that of legal certainty. Legal certainty, in reality, means that not only the sign vehicle and the meaning of the sign vehicle should be determinable, but also the legal consequences of a legally relevant factual situation, including the question whether a factual situation is legally relevant or not. Predictability presupposes a certainty relating to the sign vehicle and its meaning. To be sure, legal certainty may be regarded as a starting point of legal predictability. Neither certainty nor predictability implies the stability of a legal rule in the sense that a legal rule must exist for a relatively long time period in order to be certain and predictable. Changeableness, on the one hand, and certainty and predictability, on the other, are not necessarily conflicting terms. However, legal certainty implies the evidence of the degree of changeableness of a legal rule. Timasheff—applying the notion of probability to the problem—distinguishes "between constant and variable factors." "The constant factor" is, according to him, "perhaps only a single one, but it is decisive: This is the tendency of judges to apply the same abstract rules."[32]

Legal security implies legal certainty and an adequate legal predictability. Besides, legal security means a high probability that the legal order will be organized and operated according to the constitution. It means, therefore, that the political will as contained in the constitution and as interpreted at a certain time will be put expressly or by implication into effect without the unprovided interference of extralegal or contralegal factors. Legal security does not imply brakes against changes in exercising discretionary powers if such changes are envisaged or admitted by the legal order. It does not provide against the self-evident changing of factual situations and the changing of the meaning of sign vehicles of legal rules in the process of time. The degree of legal security is often regarded as dependent upon the establishment and functioning of certain legal institutions; as, judges independent of political and economic pressure,[33] the supervision of administrative acts by independent judges, the institution of the civil service, and, so on.

Legal security is generally envisaged as one of the

[32] *Op. cit.*, p. 316.

[33] The importance of having independent judges was recognized in ancient ages. "The Egyptian kings, according unto their law, used to swear their judges that they should not obey the king when commanded to give an unjust sentence."—Plutarch, in *Morals, The Apophthegms, or Remarkable Sayings of Kings and Other Great Commanders*, trans. by several scholars (Boston, 1871), I, 189.

foundations of social security.[34] Social security is often interpreted as implying the relative stability of certain institutions upon which a social order is based.[35] However, I suppose it is a misconception of social security to conceive it as static, contrasted to dynamic security. I cannot compare here the differences between dynamic security and political and social dynamism as treated in the political doctrine of totalitarian states.

Legal security is not a clear-cut concept. Does this deficiency indicate that it cannot be subject to reasoning? I do not think so. To "suppose that it is impossible to think logically about anything that is not clear cut"[36] has often been called an erroneous impression.

The British constitutional doctrine, to which even modern legal thinking owes so much, contains very interesting and original principles with reference to constitutional security. These principles and their reasons have been expounded by a competent authority, the Foreign Secretary of Great Britain, in the forum of the world, the Sixth Assembly of the League of Nations, September 10, 1925, before the delegates of forty-seven assembled nations. This

[34] "The general security calls for certainty, uniformity, and predictability in the adjustment of relations and regulation of conduct."— Roscoe Pound, "Individualization of Justice," 7 *Fordh. Law Rev.* 156.

[35] See Edward S. Corwin, "The Property Right Versus Legislative Power," *The Twilight of the Supreme Court* (New Haven, 1934), pp. 52 ff.

[36] See L. Susan Stebbing, *Thinking to Some Purpose* (London, 1939), p. 14.

highly significant declaration was attached to the explanation of why Great Britain declined to adopt the Protocol of October 2, 1924, providing for the Conference on Disarmament and making the League of Nations an instrument of collective security. Mr. Austen Chamberlain pointed out the position of Great Britain, stating:

"At no single moment have we formulated large general principles with a logical precision, on the contrary, nearly every vital decision that we have taken has been illogical. . . ." He called the Protocol "a code of law, a single constitution for all the states" represented in the League of Nations. "More than once," expounded Mr. Chamberlain, "at the gatherings of Ministers of the British Empire we have considered whether we might not, whether we ought not, to endeavour to put into black and white the constitution of the British Empire not as it is written but as it is practised today, and every time, and with unanimity, representatives of those different Governments have decided that, in the very elasticity which our want of logic and our want of precise definition afforded us, lay the secret of our unity and our concord." Admitting that these ideas might be strange to other nations, he continued: "It has been our practise, therefore, to eschew these large declarations of general principles, to avoid attempting to define exactly what should be done in every possible contingency that we can contemplate, knowing, as we do, that even if we provided satisfactorily for every contingency that we could contemplate, it is quite likely as not that the event which would actually happen would not conform to the exact detail of any of those which we had anticipated. We have proceeded from the particular to the general instead of from the general to the particular. We have been content to deal at any one moment with the evil of the day and to provide the remedy which that evil required."[37]

Mr. Chamberlain referred to the explanations of the acting chairman of the League of Nations, the mathematician-prime minister of France, Paul Painlevé, that the British attitude is "perhaps a consequence of those characteristics of the Anglo-Saxon mind," and that it is natural "to the Latin mind first to fix certain abstract principles, to settle general rules, and then to proceed to apply them to detailed cases."[38] This is a long passage to quote from the speech of Mr. Austen Chamberlain, but I believe that his statement is a highly expressive and sincere explanation of the British attitude toward legal and political certainty.[39] The mathematician-statesman, Painlevé, introducing the historical discussion referred to, called attention to the history of the United

[37] *Verbatim Record of the Sixth Assembly of the League of Nations,* Fifth Plenary Meeting, September 10, 1925.

[38] *Ibid.*

[39] I discussed the significance of this declaration in a paper published in 1927.

States, which has afforded "pessimists in Europe a lesson on which they cannot meditate too often." Stressing the role and the great moral authority of the American Federal Supreme Court, he contended that the American possibilities of a lasting peace can be by other countries and continents "transformed into facts by good will."[40]

We have seen that there is no clear-cut concept of legal security and of its elements, just as many elements of the concept of legal and political systems are not clear cut. The realization of this, however, should not make sterile our efforts in approaching perfection, especially as to legal security. An adequate precision in discussion and an adequate legal security (adequate to the level of our civilization) is a realizable goal that we should and can attain. Aristotle expressed the foundation of such an optimistic opinion thus: "Our discussion will be adequate if it has as much clearness as the subject-matter admits of . . ., for it is the mark of an educated man to look for precision in each class of things just so far as the nature of the subject admits."[41]

[40] *Verbatim Record of the Sixth Assembly of the League of Nations*, First Plenary Meeting, September 7, 1925.

[41] *Nicomachean Ethics*, 1094 b, *The Works of Aristotle*, trans. by W. D. Rose (Oxford, 1925), Vol. IX.

INDEX